THE BIOGRAPHY OF A TEACHER

CULTIVATING PEACEFUL EXISTENCE

YAGNESH DHORIYA

Made with ♥ on the Notion Press Platform
www.notionpress.com

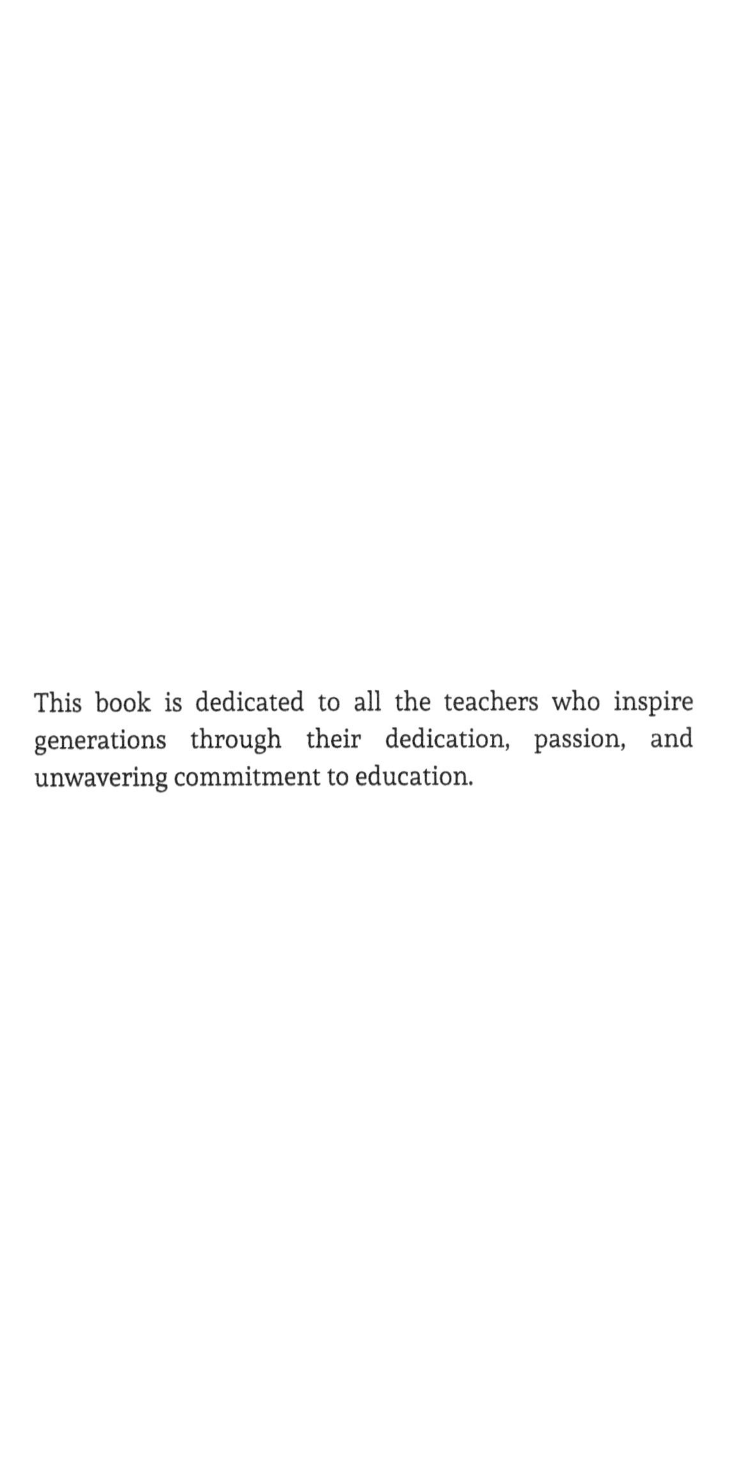

This book is dedicated to all the teachers who inspire generations through their dedication, passion, and unwavering commitment to education.

Contents

Foreword

Shree Trikamdas Ji Maharaj

Dear devotees,

Shri Naranbhai K. Dhoriya's life journey carries a divine message of devotion, dedication and compassion. Education is not limited to book knowledge alone, but is a sacred tool for shaping one's life – and Mr. Dhoriya has embodied this principle through his life.

Just as the lamp of truth and purity dispels darkness, he, as a cultured teacher and life guru, has illuminated many hearts. His life is not limited to the four walls of the classroom, but the culture he has cultivated through his compassionate teachings and inspiring deeds is a beacon of light for society.

This book is an expression of Mr. Dhoriya's life, which expresses the importance of nectar-like knowledge and selfless service. I pray at the feet of the Lord Shree Sachchidananda that every pathik who reads this book gets the opportunity to live a life of respect and may they also embark on the path of human service.

May the Almighty grant you all peace, love and light.

Shree Trikamdasji Maharaj
Mahantshree
Shree Sachchidananda Mandir
Anjar-Kachchh. Gujarat.

PREFACE

Writing this book has been a journey of discovery, reflection, and gratitude. It has provided an opportunity to delve deep into the life of an individual whose story is both unique and universal. Mr. Dhoriya represents the quintessence of what it means to be an educator, a father, and a citizen. The book not only highlights his accomplishments but also offers a glimpse into the values that have shaped his journey. His commitment to education, his empathy for others, and his ability to lead by example are qualities that inspire us all. This preface aims to provide readers with a sense of the spirit in which this biography has been written—one of admiration, respect, and deep appreciation for a life well-lived. Mr. Dhoriya is a name that resonates with profound respect and admiration within his community. He is a man whose life and character are woven together by his dedication to education, his love for his children, and his steadfast commitment to social responsibility. A combination of an excellent school teacher, an adorable father, and a great citizen, Mr. Dhoriya stands as a shining example of how one individual can positively influence multiple spheres of life.

After completing his studies, Mr. Dhoriya made the decision to become a teacher. He was eager to give back to the community that had shaped him and to influence the next generation in a way that would leave a lasting impact. His early years as a teacher were marked by hard work, perseverance, and a relentless pursuit of excellence. It wasn't long before he established a reputation for being a teacher who not only knew the subject matter inside and out but also had an innate ability to connect with his students on a personal level.

What set Mr. Dhoriya apart from other educators was his deep understanding of the diverse backgrounds and learning needs of his students. Whether he was teaching English, history, or other languages, he approached each subject with the same level of enthusiasm and dedication. His lessons were not just lectures; they were interactive experiences that encouraged critical thinking, creativity, and self-reflection. His students felt comfortable asking questions and expressing their thoughts, knowing they would be met with encouragement and respect. Mr. Dhoriya's ability to make even the most complex topics accessible was legendary. He had a gift for simplifying difficult concepts and presenting them in ways that were engaging and easy to understand. His classroom was a space where learning was not only fun but also meaningful. It was clear that for him, teaching was not a job—it was a calling.

One of Mr. Dhoriya's core beliefs was that education went beyond textbooks and exams. He was determined to instill in his students a sense of ethics, social responsibility, and empathy. He often organized extracurricular activities like debates, essay writing contests, and community service projects, encouraging his students to think critically about the world around them and to be active participants in shaping it for the better. His belief in holistic development extended beyond academic achievement; he sought to create well-rounded individuals who were not only knowledgeable but also compassionate and socially conscious. Over the years, Mr. Dhoriya's influence grew, and he became more than just a teacher. He became a mentor, a guide, and a friend to his students. Many of them sought his advice long after they had graduated, whether for academic guidance, career advice, or personal matters. His impact on his students' lives was profound, as they often cited him as the reason they pursued certain careers, developed a love for learning, or became more socially responsible individuals.

Away from the classroom, Mr. Dhoriya's role as a father was equally remarkable. He was a devoted husband and a loving father to his children. His home was a place of warmth, affection, and support—a place where his children always felt cherished and understood. While his professional life demanded a significant amount of his time and energy, Mr. Dhoriya was never one to neglect his family. He understood that the balance between work and home life was essential to the well-being of his family.

What made Mr. Dhoriya an adorable father was not just his deep love for his children but also his ability to engage with them in a way that made them feel heard and valued. He was the kind of father who took the time to listen, to understand their concerns, and to guide them through life's challenges with patience and wisdom. His children often recall how he would spend hours playing with them, telling them stories, and helping with their homework. His presence was a constant source of comfort and security. Mr. Dhoriya's approach to fatherhood was rooted in the same principles that guided his work as a teacher: patience, empathy, and respect. He believed in nurturing his children's potential while also providing them with the freedom to explore their own interests and passions. He never forced them into any particular career or path in life. Instead, he encouraged them to pursue what made them happy, knowing that success was not just about professional achievements but about personal fulfilment and happiness.

One of the most endearing qualities of Mr. Dhoriya as a father was his ability to balance discipline with warmth. He set clear boundaries and expectations for his children, but he did so with kindness and understanding. His discipline was never harsh or punitive; instead, it was focused on teaching valuable life lessons that would help them grow into responsible and compassionate individuals. His children often reflect on how he taught them the importance of honesty, hard work, and integrity—all values that would guide them through life. Perhaps the most heartwarming aspect of Mr. Dhoriya's fatherhood was his unwavering belief in the potential of his children. He always made sure they knew that they were loved, that they were enough, and that they had the power to achieve anything they set their minds to. This sense of self-worth and encouragement became the foundation for their future success, as they grew into confident, kind, and accomplished individuals.

In addition to his roles as a teacher and father, Mr. Dhoriya was also known for his outstanding contributions to his community. As a citizen, he understood the importance of giving back and worked tirelessly to improve the lives of those around him. His belief in civic responsibility was not just a theoretical ideal; it was something he lived by every day. Moreover, Mr. Dhoriya was actively involved in promoting social welfare. He often volunteered his time at local shelters and food banks, ensuring that the less fortunate in his community had access to the basic necessities of life. His compassion for those in need was evident in the countless hours he spent helping to organize community events, clean-up drives, and charity initiatives. But perhaps his most significant contribution to his community was his role as a mentor and role model. Mr. Dhoriya believed that each individual had the power to make a positive impact on the world, and he worked hard to inspire others to take action. He frequently organized seminars and talks on topics such as environmental sustainability, social justice, and the importance of community engagement. His own actions spoke louder than words, as he consistently led by example, whether it was through his work with local schools or his involvement in charity work.

His commitment to being an active and responsible citizen was reflected in the way he interacted with others. He treated everyone with respect, regardless of their background or social status. His ability to connect with people from all walks of life made him a beloved figure in his community. Whether he was participating in a community meeting, helping a neighbor with a problem, or simply offering a kind word to someone in need, Mr. Dhoriya's presence was always a source of positivity and hope. Mr. Dhoriya's legacy is one that will undoubtedly endure for generations to come. As a teacher, he helped shape the minds of countless students, inspiring them to pursue their dreams and become responsible citizens. As a father, he provided his children with the love, guidance, and support they needed to thrive. And as a citizen, he worked tirelessly to improve the community, advocating for education, social welfare, and environmental sustainability. In every aspect of his life, Mr. Dhoriya exemplifies the qualities of an exceptional teacher, a devoted father, and a responsible citizen. His story serves as a powerful reminder of the impact one person can have on the world around them. His unwavering commitment to excellence, integrity, and kindness continues to inspire those who know him, and his influence will continue to be felt for many years to come.

Now in his well-earned retirement, Mr. Dhoriya enjoys a peaceful life surrounded by his loving family and children. Though he has stepped away from the classroom, his wisdom and guidance remain readily available to those who seek it. He continues to contribute to community service, offering his time and experience whenever needed. His presence remains a source of inspiration, embodying the values he has upheld throughout his life.

Yagnesh N. Dhoriya
176-B, Mahadev Nagar
Anjar-Kachchh. Gujarat.

Acknowledgements

This book would not have been possible without the support and encouragement of many individuals. First and foremost, I extend my heartfelt gratitude to Mr. Dhoriya, whose life and teachings inspired this work. Your story is a testament to the power of education and humanity. Special thanks to my family, friends, and colleagues who offered their insights, suggestions, and unwavering support throughout the writing process, specifically Dr. Sushil Dharmani, Prof. Dharmesh Rathod, Prof. Pankaj Udeshi, Vijay Matang, Paresh Matang, Ajay Dhoriya, Anwar Hussain Rayma, Naweenchandra Maru, Bharat Matang, Kanti Dhoriya, Mahendra Bhakuni, Bharat Chavda, H Shinc and so on. Your belief in this project kept me motivated and focused. To the countless students, friends, and community members who shared their anecdotes and memories of Mr. Dhoriya, thank you for your contributions. Your stories added depth and richness to this biography. Finally, I dedicate this book to every individual who values education and seeks to make a difference in the world. May Mr. Dhoriya's story inspire you as much as it has inspired me.

INTRODUCTION

The story of Mr. Dhoriya is one that resonates with the timeless themes of resilience, sacrifice, and a profound commitment to learning and teaching. His life is a testament to the indomitable spirit of human perseverance in the face of overwhelming adversity. Born into a world of hardship in the small village of Sandhan, located in the arid Kutch District of Gujarat, Mr. Dhoriya's early years were marked by poverty and scarcity. Yet, from this humble beginning arose a story of extraordinary personal growth and social contribution that transcends the limitations of circumstance.

Mr. Dhoriya's formative years were shaped by the struggles of growing up in a large family. He was the second of ten siblings, and as the eldest son, his responsibilities and role within the family dynamics were crucial. The absence of a sister further added to the complex, patriarchal expectations placed upon him and his brothers. His parents, hardworking and determined, toiled as laborers in the fields to provide for their children. However, despite their relentless efforts, they were often at the mercy of a harsh economic reality that left them with little more than the barest essentials. The family's life was one of continuous hardship, where every meal and every necessity was earned through sheer, gruelling effort.

In the face of such a backdrop, the early death of Mr. Dhoriya's father intensified the family's struggles. His passing was a devastating blow, not just emotionally, but financially as well. In many families, the loss of a father figure can be a defining moment, one that casts a long shadow over the children's lives. Yet, for Mr. Dhoriya and his siblings, it was also a call to action, a catalyst that would drive them to find strength in their mother, who, despite the overwhelming loss, rose to the occasion. With unshakeable determination, she assumed both maternal and paternal roles, becoming the anchor of the family. She was not only a mother but also a teacher, instilling in her children a sense of resilience, duty, and the importance of education as a means of overcoming life's challenges.

Her sacrifices were numerous, and every ounce of her energy was devoted to ensuring that her children had the opportunity to rise above their circumstances. In her eyes, education was the golden key that could unlock the doors to a brighter future. She imbued her sons with a sense of responsibility—each of them understood that their education was not merely for their personal advancement but for the collective good of the family and, eventually, the community. Mr. Dhoriya's mother was the embodiment of love in action, a living example of how dedication and selflessness can transcend the hardships of life. Her steadfastness and courage became a guiding light for Mr. Dhoriya and his brothers, helping them navigate the murky waters of early adulthood.

As the eldest sibling, Mr. Dhoriya's life was also deeply influenced by the sacrifices of his older brother, who, recognizing the potential for a better future through education, made the heart-wrenching decision to forgo his own dreams. The older brother's sacrifice—choosing to take up manual labor to support Mr. Dhoriya's studies—was a defining moment for the entire family. It was an act of generosity that demanded a response, a response that would be shaped by gratitude and responsibility. Mr. Dhoriya, fully aware of the enormity of this sacrifice, became more determined than ever to honor it. His brother's unspoken belief in him was a driving force, pushing him to work tirelessly toward his academic goals. This profound sense of duty toward his family, particularly to the brother who had put his own future on hold for his sake, would shape Mr. Dhoriya's character and his future achievements.

Despite the many obstacles that stood in his way, Mr. Dhoriya's academic potential became evident early on. Though his circumstances were far from ideal, he excelled in his studies, a testament to his innate intelligence and, perhaps more importantly, to his unyielding perseverance. The narrowness of his economic situation did not stifle his intellectual curiosity; instead, it served as a crucible that forged his character. With each passing day, he worked tirelessly to overcome the financial constraints that could have so easily impeded his academic progress. Every textbook was a treasure, every moment of study a victory against the odds.

Mr. Dhoriya's commitment to education led him to pursue higher learning, and it was through his relentless dedication that he eventually earned both a Master of Arts (MA) and a Bachelor of Education (B.Ed.) in English Literature. These achievements were not merely academic triumphs; they were symbols of the collective sacrifice of his family, a tribute to his mother's unwavering faith and his brother's selflessness. His decision to study English Literature, a field both intellectually demanding and deeply rewarding, further illustrated his thirst for knowledge and his desire to engage with ideas that could foster change in both his own life and the lives of others. It was a field that would allow him to connect with a broader world, one that could transcend the geographic and social limitations of his rural upbringing.

In many ways, Mr. Dhoriya's academic success was more than a personal victory; it was a reflection of the values instilled in him by his family. It symbolized the power of education not only as a means of personal advancement but as a tool for social mobility. His success proved that talent and determination, when coupled with the right opportunities, could break through the shackles of poverty. His story is a reminder that individuals are not defined solely by their circumstances, but by their ability to navigate them and, in doing so, forge paths that inspire others.

After completing his formal education, Mr. Dhoriya embarked on a career that would allow him to share his knowledge and experience with others. His journey into the world of education was not an easy one. At first, he worked as a clerk, balancing the demands of a full-time job with his academic aspirations. It was a juggling act that required immense discipline and time management skills, yet he never wavered in his commitment to both his personal and professional growth. Even as he faced the pressures of work, the weight of his familial responsibilities, and the difficulties of life in a small village, Mr. Dhoriya continued to push forward, relentlessly pursuing his dream of becoming an educator.

As he progressed in his career, his dedication to teaching and to uplifting his community became increasingly apparent. Mr. Dhoriya's rise to prominence was not through any single grand gesture but through his steady, consistent efforts to make a difference in the lives of those around him. His work as an educator was rooted in the belief that knowledge had the power to transform lives, and that by imparting education, he could offer others the same opportunities that had enabled him to escape the constraints of his humble beginnings. Each lesson he taught was an opportunity not just for academic growth, but for personal empowerment. In this way, Mr. Dhoriya's teaching was never just about books or grades; it was about instilling a sense of possibility, hope, and confidence in his students.

Mr. Dhoriya's influence extended beyond the classroom. He became a mentor, a guide, and a role model for countless individuals who, like him, came from difficult circumstances but believed in the transformative power of education. His life story is a powerful reminder of the profound impact that one dedicated individual can have on the lives of others. He was, and continues to be, a beacon of hope for those who may otherwise have been overlooked or forgotten by society. His work as a teacher was a testament to the belief that education is not merely about the transmission of knowledge, but about shaping lives, empowering individuals, and inspiring future generations to strive for something greater.

Amidst a culture that frequently underestimates the value of education, where access to resources can be limited, and where inequality continues to persist, Mr.

Dhoriya's journey stands as an enduring example of the power of perseverance, familial support, and an unwavering commitment to one's purpose. His story not only exemplifies the potential of individuals to overcome their circumstances but also serves as a beacon for those who might be facing their own struggles. It is a reminder that, with dedication, determination, and the support of others, even the most difficult of beginnings can be transformed into a story of success, growth, and lasting impact.

In every corner of his life, Mr. Dhoriya has demonstrated that the pursuit of knowledge and the dedication to teaching are not merely personal endeavors but are, in fact, acts of service to humanity. His life continues to inspire generations of students and educators, and it is a story that will remain relevant as long as the pursuit of education and the betterment of society remain central to our shared human endeavor. His legacy, rooted in the sacrifices of his family and his own tireless efforts, will continue to illuminate the path for future generations who dare to dream beyond their immediate circumstances and seek a better, brighter future through education.

I

Empathy

"If what I say resonates with you, it's merely because we're branches of the same tree."
—**William Butler Yeats**

Empathy, that most delicate yet potent of human virtues, is frequently described as the ability to not only understand the emotions and experiences of others but to share in them. In its truest form, empathy transcends mere intellectual comprehension, entering the realm of emotional resonance, where one's heart beats in synchrony with another's. For Mr. Mr. Dhoriya, empathy was not simply a noble trait but the very axis around which his life spun. It was woven into the fabric of his relationships with students, peers, and strangers alike, making his every interaction an embodiment of compassionate understanding. His life stands as a testament to the profound impact that simple acts of empathy can have in shaping the lives of those around him.

Mr. Dhoriya's approach to empathy was not merely theoretical or philosophical. It was embodied in the quiet, consistent ways he engaged with the world. His ability to respond to the pain, joy, or confusion of others with an open heart and mind turned his life into a series of small, yet transformative, ripples. Each of these ripples, though seemingly inconsequential in isolation, accumulated over time to form a legacy that would extend far beyond his years, touching generations in ways he may never have fully realized.

A Father's Compassionate Lie

The relationship between a parent and a child is one of the most intimate and sacred bonds in human experience, built upon a foundation of unconditional love, support, and sacrifice. But this bond is rarely free from complexity. It is often characterized by unspoken burdens, silent compromises, and moments of deep, existential reflection. Mr. Dhoriya's role as a father was no exception, yet it was marked by a singular quality that defined his character: empathy.

One such instance illustrates his remarkable capacity for understanding beyond his own pride. When his son's board exam results were announced, the marks were modest, revealing a score of only 40%. To the outside world, this might have been seen as a failure—a shortcoming to be lamented or criticized. But for Mr. Dhoriya, this result was not a reflection of his son's worth but a measure of his effort, perseverance, and dedication. He felt no shame, only pride in his child's struggle and growth.

However, when conversing with a close friend whose son had barely passed, securing the minimum marks required, Mr. Dhoriya chose a different approach. Instead of offering words that might deepen his friend's disappointment or sense of failure, he chose to protect his friend's emotional well-being. "I understand what you're going through," he said gently, "My son, too, only managed to scrape through with 35%."

This seemingly minor alteration—this small untruth—speaks volumes about Mr. Dhoriya's empathy. It was not a lie born out of malice or a desire to distort the truth, but rather an act of profound understanding. He recognized that, in that moment, what his friend needed was not the cold comfort of reality but the warm reassurance that his own son's struggles were not unique or isolating. The words, though false, shifted the narrative from one of comparison to one of shared human experience. Mr. Dhoriya placed the emotional well-being of his friend above his own pride, choosing connection over personal advantage. In this simple act, he demonstrated that empathy does not require grand gestures, but it does require a willingness to prioritize another's needs over one's own ego.

The Brotherhood of Grief

Grief is one of the most isolating human experiences, a universal emotion that, paradoxically, can make us feel more alone than ever. When a loved one passes, it is not only the absence of the person that we mourn but the profound sense of dislocation that accompanies their departure. The experience of loss can fracture one's world, rendering even the simplest of tasks insurmountable. In the face of such deep sorrow, it is not the words of comfort that matter most but the mere presence of another human being, offering silent companionship and understanding.

Mr. Dhoriya's response to the grief of a close friend who had lost his wife at an early age exemplifies the profound power of empathy during moments of profound loss. The suddenness and finality of death can often leave survivors in a state of shock, their emotions in disarray. In such moments, what one needs most is not advice or solutions but a shoulder to lean on—someone who will sit with them in their sorrow, offering silent solidarity. Mr. Dhoriya recognized this instinctively.

For twelve consecutive days, he visited his grieving friend, offering not words but the comfort of consistent, compassionate presence. He did not attempt to "fix" his friend's pain or offer platitudes that might feel hollow in the face of such overwhelming loss. Instead, he simply sat with him, listened to his grief, and allowed the space for sorrow to be expressed without judgment. He treated his friend not as an acquaintance but as a brother, and in doing so, he showed that true empathy involves being present with another person's pain, even when there is nothing that can be done to alleviate it.

Through his actions, Mr. Dhoriya communicated a powerful truth: empathy is not about the desire to solve problems or provide answers. It is about offering a space where another person can simply be, without the need for explanation or justification. His quiet companionship was a balm for his friend's wounded soul, reminding him that in the most difficult moments, one is never truly alone.

Calm in the Face of Misunderstanding

Empathy, however, is not solely tested in moments of sorrow and loss; it is equally, if not more, crucial in times of misunderstanding and conflict. It is easy to be compassionate when the world is calm, when the emotional temperature is low, but the true test of empathy comes when tempers flare, when words are spoken in haste, and when anger clouds the judgment of both parties.

One such moment came when Mr. Dhoriya and his wife were unjustly criticized by a widow whose children he had taught free of charge, without expectation of recompense. This woman, clearly overwhelmed by the burdens of widowhood and the weight of her personal struggles, lashed out at the very person who had offered her family a hand of kindness. Her outburst was not about Mr. Dhoriya or his wife; it was a reflection of her own deep-seated pain, frustration, and helplessness.

Rather than retaliating in kind or defending himself, Mr. Dhoriya responded with remarkable composure. He understood that her words, though harsh, were not intended to wound him personally. "Her words are not about us," he later explained to his wife. "They are about her. Her struggles. Her pain. If we can't absorb that, who will?"

This response encapsulates the essence of empathy. In the face of a potentially hurtful situation, Mr. Dhoriya chose to look beyond the surface, recognizing the deep emotional currents that influenced the widow's behavior. He refrained from engaging in defensive posturing or attempting to prove his own righteousness. Instead, he chose to meet her pain with understanding, absorbing her anger as a reflection of her internal struggles. This, too, is a profound lesson in the quiet strength of empathy—not to take offense, but to see beyond the words, to the heart of the matter.

Small Gestures, Big Impacts

The many anecdotes of Mr. Dhoriya's empathetic acts may seem, at first glance, like small, isolated instances of kindness. Yet when taken together, they reveal a man who lived a life rooted in others' welfare, whose every action was guided by an unwavering sense of humanity. Whether it was the way he spoke to his students, the manner in which he comforted his friends, or the countless silent acts of understanding he extended to strangers, Mr. Dhoriya's empathy was not a fleeting sentiment but a way of being.

He didn't just teach his students the rules of grammar or the intricacies of English literature. He taught them, through his very presence, how to navigate the world with kindness and understanding. His ability to perceive the struggles of those around him, often before they were voiced, set him apart as a teacher not merely of academic subjects but of life itself. He instilled in his students a deep respect for the power of empathy, showing them that the true measure of a person's character is not in their achievements or accolades, but in their ability to connect with others on a human level.

A Legacy of Understanding

Empathy is, above all else, contagious. The people who are touched by it often carry its lessons forward, sharing the spirit of understanding with those they encounter. Mr. Dhoriya's life, marked by countless acts of quiet kindness, has left an indelible imprint on the hearts of those who knew him. His legacy is not only in the lessons he taught or the knowledge he imparted, but in the ripple effect of compassion he set in motion.

Amid a society that frequently values competition, self-interest, and material success, Mr. Dhoriya's life serves as a reminder of the transformative power of empathy. It is a quiet strength, one that can heal wounds, bridge divides, and inspire generations. His story teaches us that the smallest gestures—words of comfort, moments of presence, acts of understanding—can have an outsized impact, shaping lives in ways we may never fully comprehend.

In the end, the legacy of Mr. Dhoriya is not one of accolades or public recognition, but one of deeply human connections forged through the power of empathy. His life is a living testament to the enduring truth that the greatest impact we can have in this world is not through grand gestures or monumental achievements, but through the simple, profound act of understanding another person's heart.

II
Intuitiveness

"The only real valuable thing is intuition."
—Albert Einstein

In a society that often values external achievements more than internal balance, Mr. Dhoriya's life stands as a steadfast example of the power of intuition. Where many rushed toward the material pursuits of wealth, power, and status, he chose instead a path of simplicity, spiritual grounding, and a deep, unwavering trust in his inner voice. His life, unencumbered by the frenetic chase for worldly success, was guided by a force that transcended reason and analysis—his profound sense of intuition. This intuitive wisdom, for Mr. Dhoriya, was not merely a passive trait but an active guide, shaping decisions, relationships, and his very philosophy of life.

In his quiet yet profound way, Mr. Dhoriya demonstrated that true peace and contentment are not derived from external accomplishments or possessions but from the ability to listen deeply to one's inner compass. His life, in many ways, serves as an antidote to the noise and distractions of modern living, offering a clear and serene alternative to the stress-filled pursuit of material success. By following his intuitive understanding, Mr. Dhoriya proved that peace of mind, grounded in simplicity and spiritual awareness, is the truest form of wealth.

A Life Free from the Temptations of Materialism

The modern world bombards us with endless advertisements, social pressures, and societal expectations that push us toward the relentless accumulation of wealth and status. In such an environment, the pursuit of material gain becomes almost a default setting for many individuals. Stock markets, real estate, and speculative ventures, often celebrated as gateways to prosperity, seduce the masses into the pursuit of fleeting riches. These temptations can overshadow the more subtle, intangible values that bring lasting satisfaction and fulfillment.

Yet for Mr. Dhoriya, this ever-present allure of materialism held no sway. He did not seek the allure of speculative investments or the promise of fleeting riches. He was not drawn into the high-stakes world of financial transactions or the fast-paced competition for more possessions. Instead, he lived a life in contrast to the consumerist hustle that defined so much of contemporary society. His decision to remain untouched by the rampant materialism around him was not rooted in ignorance or naiveté, but in a deep understanding of the true cost of such pursuits.

Mr. Dhoriya had observed the lives of those who had thrown themselves into the race for material wealth. He saw how their lives became ensnared in a cycle of anxiety and dissatisfaction, always reaching for the next financial goal, only to find that with each achievement, the sense of fulfillment grew more elusive. The chase for more—more money, more property, more status—seemed to offer temporary satisfaction, but it was often followed by stress, fear, and exhaustion. In contrast, Mr. Dhoriya found true richness not in material abundance, but in the inner peace that could not be shaken by external circumstances.

While many of his peers were caught in the turmoil of striving for more, he chose contentment with what he had, finding wealth not in the quantity of possessions but in the quality of his emotional and spiritual life. He understood, with a clarity that few could match, that material wealth was fleeting. The lasting value, he realized, was to be found in the cultivation of one's inner world, where true peace and fulfillment reside.

Trusting Intuition and Spiritual Guidance

At the core of Mr. Dhoriya's approach to life lay a deeply-rooted sense of intuition—a quiet yet persistent voice within that guided him through life's myriad challenges. His intuition was not some mystical or unexplained phenomenon, but rather the result of years of mindfulness, self-awareness, and spiritual practice. His sense of inner knowing allowed him to navigate the complexities of life with calm and wisdom, grounded in spiritual principles that emphasized peace over profit, clarity over confusion, and contentment over desire.

Surrounded by the constant barrage of external noise, Mr. Dhoriya's ability to listen to his inner voice was nothing short of remarkable. His decisions were not swayed by the rapid shifts of market forces or the pressures of society. Instead, he trusted his intuition to guide him toward the paths that would preserve his peace of mind and spiritual well-being. This was evident in his approach to financial matters. Where others might have rushed into investments driven by greed or external pressures, he chose instead to wait, plan, and act only when he felt certain that his choices were in alignment with his deeper values.

Mr. Dhoriya's reliance on intuition also extended beyond material pursuits. In his personal life, he trusted his inner wisdom to shape the way he interacted with others. Whether in his relationships with friends, colleagues, or family, he approached every interaction with an openness and mindfulness that reflected his spiritual clarity. He understood that decisions driven by intuition were decisions grounded in a deeper truth, one that transcended the fleeting desires of the ego and connected him to a higher sense of purpose.

Observing the Lives of Others

Mr. Dhoriya's deep sense of intuition was further honed by his acute powers of observation. He was an astute listener, carefully watching and learning from the lives of those around him. Through careful observation, he began to see the often-unspoken consequences of material pursuits on the lives of his friends and peers. Many of those around him, driven by the belief that success could be quantified in terms of wealth and possessions, found themselves ensnared in a constant cycle of stress, worry, and burnout.

Despite their financial achievements, these individuals were often emotionally drained, struggling with sleepless nights, constant anxiety, and an overwhelming sense of dissatisfaction. Their lives, filled with external signs of success, lacked the one thing Mr. Dhoriya valued above all: peace. He understood that the pursuit of material wealth, when driven by external pressures and societal expectations, often led to emotional exhaustion and spiritual disconnection.

In contrast to his peers, Mr. Dhoriya chose a life that emphasized simplicity, patience, and spiritual fulfillment. He knew that true success was not found in the accumulation of assets, but in the ability to live a life that was free from unnecessary stress and distraction. His peers, though outwardly successful, were caught in a never-ending cycle of striving for more. They believed that happiness was just one more purchase away, yet no matter how much they attained, the feeling of contentment always seemed just beyond their grasp.

Through his intuitive understanding of life's rhythms, Mr. Dhoriya knew that true contentment could never be bought. It could only be cultivated within, through spiritual practice, mindfulness, and the cultivation of inner peace.

The Practice of Living Simply

Perhaps one of the most striking aspects of Mr. Dhoriya's life was his commitment to simplicity. He believed that a simple life was the key to mental clarity and emotional stability. This simplicity was not limited to the material aspects of his life, but extended to every aspect of his being. He lived within his means, always careful not to exceed his resources, and he believed that true wealth lay not in what one could accumulate but in what one could let go.

This simplicity also extended to his relationships. Unlike many people who sought validation or recognition through their social status, Mr. Dhoriya valued authenticity above all else. He sought not superficial interactions but deep, meaningful connections with those around him. He believed that true friendship, love, and connection could not be purchased or manufactured—they were the result of sincerity, kindness, and mutual respect.

In a society fueled by consumerism and the quest for material recognition, Mr. Dhoriya's humility and simplicity offered a refreshing reminder that true worth lies not in what one owns, but in the character one nurtures.His life was a living example of how true richness comes not from the accumulation of things, but from the cultivation of inner peace and authenticity.

Living by Spiritual Principles, Not Material Ones

While many in Mr. Dhoriya's world made decisions based on material desires—purchasing items to impress others or making investments to secure a future defined by societal expectations—he chose to live by spiritual principles. For him, peace of mind, emotional stability, and integrity were the guiding forces that determined the course of his life. His intuition was deeply attuned to these values, allowing him to make decisions that were in harmony with his deeper purpose.

In every aspect of his life—whether in his financial dealings, his personal relationships, or his approach to work—Mr. Dhoriya remained grounded in the principles of spiritual growth and inner peace. He understood that true success did not come from external achievements or possessions, but from the ability to remain calm, centered, and grounded, regardless of the circumstances.

His approach to life was a powerful reminder that happiness and contentment are not found in the accumulation of wealth, but in the alignment of one's life with their deeper values. By living in harmony with his intuition, Mr. Dhoriya created a life that was rich in meaning, purpose, and inner peace.

The Gift of Peaceful Decision-Making

Through his intuitive approach to life, Mr. Dhoriya demonstrated that peace of mind is the greatest gift one can attain. He made decisions based not on the demands of society or the pressures of material success, but on a deep, inner wisdom that prioritized spiritual clarity and emotional well-being. By resisting the temptations of materialism, choosing to live simply, and trusting his intuition, he crafted a life that was calm, purposeful, and fulfilling.

Often equating success with financial gain and outward appearances, Mr. Dhoriya's life serves as a quiet yet powerful testament to the value of spiritual wisdom, simplicity, and intuitive decision-making.His ability to live a life free from the pressures of materialism, while remaining deeply connected to his inner peace, is a legacy that continues to inspire all who had the privilege of knowing him. Through his example, we are reminded that true wealth is found not in external possessions but in the peace, clarity, and contentment that arise from living a life grounded in intuition and spiritual truth.

III
Passion

Mr. Dhoriya's passion for physical fitness is not just a lifelong commitment—it is a central and defining aspect of his existence. From a young age, this passion shaped his life in profound ways, creating a foundation of vitality and energy that continues to influence his health and well-being. While many may begin to slow down as they age, Mr. Dhoriya has remained resolute in his devotion to maintaining a level of physical fitness that exceeds expectations for his age. His passion for staying fit is not just a personal goal; it is a reflection of his core values and philosophies on life.

Early Passion for Sports

The roots of Mr. Dhoriya's passion for physical activity began in his childhood, where cricket, India's beloved national sport, captured his heart with unrelenting enthusiasm. The fields of his village were his stage, where he honed his skills, developed friendships, and immersed himself in the excitement of competition. Cricket wasn't just a sport to Mr. Dhoriya—it was an outlet for his boundless energy, a place to forge connections, and a symbol of his youthful vigor.

For him, each match was not just about playing but about pushing his body to its limits, sharpening his skills, and constantly striving to improve. Whether it was the thrill of hitting a boundary or the mental challenge of outsmarting an opponent, the sport fueled his sense of accomplishment and joy. The sport was his escape and his motivation, becoming a central thread that connected him to something larger than his immediate circumstances. As he played, he didn't just enjoy the game; he was living and breathing it, lost in the intensity of each moment.

As the years passed, responsibilities began to accumulate, and the demands of life shifted. Yet, Mr. Dhoriya's love for physical activity remained. At the age of 50, he made the decision to shift from cricket to a new sport—volleyball. This transition wasn't forced, but rather a natural evolution—a desire to embrace a new challenge. Volleyball reignited his competitive spirit, offering a different kind of excitement, one centered around teamwork, strategy, and endurance.

The Shift to Volleyball and Lifelong Dedication to Fitness

While many might consider stepping away from competitive sports in their 50s, Mr. Dhoriya's passion for staying physically active remained just as strong. Instead of slowing down, he embraced volleyball with the same intensity and enthusiasm that he had once given cricket. As he delved into the sport, Mr. Dhoriya was able to push his body in ways he had never imagined, all while remaining mentally sharp. The game's strategic nature demanded quick thinking, alertness, and precision—qualities that not only kept him physically fit but also enhanced his cognitive health.

His commitment to fitness became an inspiration to those around him. As he entered his 60s, Mr. Dhoriya defied the typical expectations of aging, proving that vitality and physical fitness were not just for the young. His determination to stay active became a powerful reminder that age is no barrier to living a healthy and dynamic life. Mr. Dhoriya embraced the idea that the older you become, the more essential it is to prioritize your health. For him, fitness wasn't a vanity project—it was a necessity, essential not just for personal well-being but for his ability to care for his family. Physical fitness, he understood, was the foundation of a strong, engaged, and productive life.

Walking, Cycling, and Staying Active

Even as Mr. Dhoriya's years advanced, his commitment to physical activity remained unshaken. Walking became one of his primary forms of exercise in his 60s. Each day, without fail, he would walk at least five kilometers through the scenic and peaceful gardens of Anjar. For Mr. Dhoriya, walking was more than just physical exercise—it was a sacred ritual. The rhythmic cadence of his steps provided him with time for reflection, mental clarity, and a deeper connection to nature. The tranquility of his surroundings became a form of meditation, a calming influence that grounded him and allowed him to clear his mind.

What is truly remarkable about Mr. Dhoriya's approach to exercise is his consistency. Amid countless distractions and excuses, Mr. Dhoriya's daily commitment to walking stands as a testament to his discipline. Whether walking through the gardens or cycling along the quiet lanes of his village, Mr. Dhoriya has never wavered in his dedication to staying active. The act of walking five kilometers is more than a simple routine—it is a reflection of his deep, unyielding commitment to his health and well-being.

Cycling, too, has become an integral part of his lifestyle. The joy and freedom he experiences when riding his bike—the wind in his face, the feeling of being outdoors—are essential elements of his ongoing vitality. His well-maintained bicycle symbolizes his commitment to staying healthy and active, whether he is cycling for leisure or exercise. For Mr. Dhoriya, cycling represents both a means of physical activity and a connection to a sense of freedom and joy.

Avoiding the Pitfalls of Modern Life

Mr. Dhoriya's passion for physical fitness has also served as a safeguard against many of the pitfalls of modern life. In an age where unhealthy habits like smoking, drinking, and overeating are prevalent, Mr.

Dhoriya has remained immune to such distractions. His love for fitness has kept him focused, disciplined, and immune to the vices that have claimed the health of many others. Unlike many of his peers who gather at local tea stalls to indulge in unhealthy habits, Mr. Dhoriya has never allowed such temptations to take root in his life.

This remarkable resilience can be attributed to his passion for staying fit—a passion that has motivated him to stay away from unhealthy practices. His unwavering dedication to physical activity has kept him mentally and physically strong, enabling him to avoid the consequences of indulgence and to live a long, healthy, and vibrant life.

An Example of Independence and Self-Reliance

One of the most inspiring aspects of Mr. Dhoriya's life is his complete self-reliance. He is never one to ask for help, regardless of how small the task. An incident that perfectly illustrates this quality occurred when his bike ran out of fuel. Rather than waiting for someone to assist him, Mr. Dhoriya simply dragged the bike back to the garage, demonstrating his innate ability to handle challenges independently. This wasn't an act of pride but of self-sufficiency—a key characteristic of Mr. Dhoriya's personality.

This self-reliance extends far beyond physical tasks. It reflects a larger philosophy of life—that a man's true strength lies in his ability to stand on his own. Mr. Dhoriya's life has been built on a foundation of self-discipline, resilience, and a commitment to self-improvement. These values have guided him through countless challenges, helping him remain grounded and focused on what truly matters.

The Supreme Importance of Health

For Mr. Dhoriya, health is the single most important asset one can possess. He understands that without good health, it is impossible to contribute to others, to support family and community, or to live a meaningful life. His commitment to staying fit is not just for his own benefit—it is a gift he gives to his family. He believes that the healthier he is, the longer he will be able to care for and support his loved ones.

As a teacher and mentor, Mr. Dhoriya has demonstrated how the pursuit of health can lead to a life of purpose and fulfillment. Unlike many of his peers who show signs of physical decline, Mr. Dhoriya's continued energy, vitality, and enthusiasm serve as a living example of what is possible when one places a priority on physical well-being. His ability to remain youthful, energetic, and present is a reflection of his deep commitment to health, and it continues to inspire all those around him.

A Legacy of Passion and Vitality

At the age of 62, Mr. Dhoriya's life remains a powerful testament to the importance of passion, discipline, and commitment to living a full, healthy life. His dedication to staying fit—whether through daily walks, cycling, or engaging in sports—is a shining example of how passion for one's health can transcend age. Mr. Dhoriya has demonstrated that with the right mindset and commitment, age is no barrier to living a life full of vitality, energy, and purpose.

His story is a legacy of passion and vitality, inspiring anyone who believes that age should slow them down. With determination, passion, and a focus on health, one can remain as strong, vibrant, and youthful as ever—no matter how many years pass. Mr. Dhoriya's unwavering commitment to fitness continues to be an inspiration to all who know him, reminding us that passion for life is timeless.

IV
A Life-long Learning

"Anyone who stops learning is old, whether at twenty or eighty. Anyone who keeps learning stays young."
—Henry Ford

Mr. Dhoriya's life has been a testament to the power of education and the unyielding drive to learn, regardless of the circumstances. His journey of learning began at a young age, but it was not a straightforward path. It was one filled with challenges, sacrifices, and a deep sense of purpose. What truly sets Mr. Dhoriya apart is not just his thirst for knowledge but his ability to adapt, evolve, and continue learning throughout his life. From the moment he picked up his first book at the age of eight, to his later academic achievements, Mr. Dhoriya's pursuit of education never ceased, even when life seemed determined to throw obstacles in his way.

Early Beginnings: The Struggles of Starting Late

Born into a family with nine brothers and no sisters, Mr. Dhoriya's early life in the small, rural village of Sandhan, located in Naliya Taluka of Kachchh District, Gujarat, was one of scarcity and hardship. Like many children in such environments, Mr. Dhoriya's initial exposure to education was delayed. While most children start their formal schooling by the age of six, Mr. Dhoriya's journey began at the age of eight.

This delay, however, was not due to any lack of intelligence or ability. Rather, it was a reflection of the harsh realities of rural life, where access to education was a privilege, not a given. His father, a hardworking laborer, did his best to provide for his large family, but resources were always limited. When Mr. Dhoriya's father passed away at an early age, the family's situation became even more difficult. His mother, a pillar of strength, had to shoulder the responsibility of raising her sons on her own. In this atmosphere of adversity, Mr. Dhoriya's educational journey took on a more significant meaning.

At the age of eight, Mr. Dhoriya learned the alphabet of the English language. This was no simple feat, considering the circumstances. In an environment where formal education was often secondary to the pressing need for survival, the very act of beginning to learn at this age was a statement of resilience. He knew that education was the key to a better future, not just for himself but for his family as well. And though the world around him often seemed to be working against him, he was determined to prove that no matter the age, no matter the starting point, learning could always be the way forward.

Overcoming Obstacles: The Will to Succeed

While his formal education began late, Mr. Dhoriya's commitment to learning was unwavering. His passion for knowledge was clear from the beginning, as he quickly became an eager student. Despite the challenges he faced, including the scarcity of resources, he excelled in his studies. One of the most significant obstacles he faced was the lack of proper lighting to study at night. In a small village like Sandhan, electricity was a rare luxury. As a result, Mr. Dhoriya had to use a lantern to study after sunset—a task that was not only difficult but also dangerous in the absence of proper lighting.

However, this never deterred him. His resolve was stronger than the challenges he faced. The flickering light of the lantern may have made reading and writing more challenging, but it also ignited a fire within him—a fire to prove that no circumstance, no matter how difficult, could stand in the way of his education. This determination led to remarkable achievements, as Mr. Dhoriya became one of the few individuals in his village to complete his 10th-grade board exams with bright marks.

In a small village like Sandhan, completing the 10th grade was not a small accomplishment. For many, education stopped after elementary school, and the lack of resources meant that higher education was a distant dream. Yet Mr. Dhoriya's dedication to learning turned this dream into a reality. He became an inspiration to his peers, a living proof that despite the most challenging conditions, progress was possible if one had the willpower and determination to achieve it.

Being the second-born in a family of nine brothers, Mr. Dhoriya's achievement was even more significant. In a family where many of his siblings had to abandon their education early to work and support the family, Mr. Dhoriya's completion of his 10th board exam marked him as an outlier. His perseverance made him the only one in his family who managed to pursue higher studies, further solidifying the importance he placed on education. This accomplishment was not just a personal victory; it was a victory for his entire family, a testimony to the sacrifices and hard work that his mother, and even his siblings, had invested in his future.

A Turning Point: The Influence of a Mentor

While Mr. Dhoriya's academic journey had many challenges, it was also marked by moments of profound learning and growth. One such moment came when he was in the 9th grade. At this point in his life, Mr. Dhoriya was beginning to stray from his academic path. As a young teenager, he found himself distracted by the world outside the classroom. However, it was at this pivotal moment that he encountered a mentor who would change his life.

Versibhai Maheshwari, the warden of the hostel Mr. Dhoriya stayed at, reprimanded him for deviating from his studies. The scolding was stern and intense, but it had a profound effect on Mr. Dhoriya. He understood the seriousness of his situation and the immense opportunity that education presented. The reprimand, though harsh, became a turning point in his life. It woke him up to the realization that his future was in his own hands and that he had to work harder than ever before if he was to succeed.

From that moment on, Mr. Dhoriya committed himself wholeheartedly to his studies. His dedication became evident, and his grades reflected the hard work and determination that he poured into his education. This lesson in discipline and focus would stay with him for the rest of his life, serving as a constant reminder that learning was not a passive endeavor—it required hard work, commitment, and, at times, difficult sacrifices.

The Dream Job: Becoming a Teacher

After completing his 10th board exams with distinction, Mr. Dhoriya's academic journey was far from over. While many of his peers were content with their education, Mr. Dhoriya knew that he wanted more. His dream was to become a teacher—an English teacher, to be precise. In a rural village like Sandhan, the opportunity to teach English was rare, and Mr. Dhoriya's ambition stood out as an anomaly. However, his dedication to learning and his innate passion for the English language propelled him forward.

Mr. Dhoriya's first professional job was as a clerk in the State Government. It was a stable position, one that provided him with financial security, but it was not his dream job. The dream of becoming an English teacher remained in the back of his mind, burning quietly but persistently. In 1989, after years of hard work, perseverance, and self-discipline, Mr. Dhoriya achieved his dream. He was appointed as an English teacher, a position that not only fulfilled his personal aspirations but also allowed him to contribute to the educational growth of others.

Becoming a teacher was not just a professional achievement for Mr. Dhoriya; it was the culmination of a lifelong journey of learning. He had always been a student at heart, and now, as a teacher, he could pass on the knowledge he had acquired to others. Mr. Dhoriya became a beacon of hope and inspiration for his students. His journey, from a young boy studying by the light of a lantern to becoming a teacher, spoke volumes about the power of persistence, resilience, and the thirst for knowledge.

A Dream Fulfilled: The Pursuit of a Master's Degree

Despite achieving his dream job, there was one part of Mr. Dhoriya's education that still eluded him: a Master's degree in English. When he was younger, circumstances had made it impossible for him to pursue higher education. But as a lifelong learner, Mr. Dhoriya never gave up on this dream. His passion for learning never dulled, and he remained committed to fulfilling this unfinished chapter of his academic journey.

The opportunity to finally earn his Master's degree came unexpectedly. When his elder son, Yagnesh, began studying for his MA in English, Mr. Dhoriya saw it as the perfect opportunity to fulfill his own dream. He enrolled in the same program and, in doing so, showed his son—and the world—that learning never stops, no matter the age.

Mr. Dhoriya's pursuit of his Master's degree was not just a personal achievement; it was a powerful statement about the importance of lifelong learning. It was a lesson that age should never be a barrier to education, and that the pursuit of knowledge should never cease, regardless of the stage of life one is in.

A Legacy of Lifelong Learning

Mr. Dhoriya's story is a powerful reminder that learning is a lifelong endeavor, one that never truly ends. From his humble beginnings in Sandhan to becoming a teacher and earning his Master's degree, Mr. Dhoriya's journey exemplifies the transformative power of education. His life serves as an inspiration to others, showing that no matter where you start, no matter the obstacles you face, a commitment to learning can change the course of your life.

For Mr. Dhoriya, education was never just about acquiring knowledge—it was about the values it instilled in him. It taught him resilience, discipline, and the importance of giving back to others. As a teacher, he passed these lessons on to his students, leaving a legacy of knowledge, compassion, and a passion for lifelong learning.

His story continues to inspire not just his family but all those who hear it. Mr. Dhoriya's life is proof that learning is not just a phase but a continuous journey—a journey that can change lives and open doors to new possibilities, no matter when you begin.

V

Persuasion

"Thaw with his gentle persuasion is more powerful than Thor with his hammer. The one melts, the other breaks into pieces."
– Henry D. Thoreau

Mr. Dhoriya's life was a testament to the power of persuasion, not through force or manipulation, but through a deep, unwavering belief in the goodness of people and the transformative power of words. He had a unique ability to convince, to change minds, and to bring out the best in others, often at times when they least expected it. His influence reached far beyond the classroom, where he was known as one of the most respected and admired teachers in town. But it was not just his knowledge that earned him this reverence—it was his remarkable ability to connect with people, regardless of their background, their station in life, or their personal struggles.

Mr. Dhoriya's persuasion was rooted in his integrity and his genuine care for those around him. His words carried weight because they were always spoken with the intent to help, guide, and support. He never sought to dominate a conversation or force an opinion. Instead, he listened intently, carefully considering the situation, before offering his advice. His approach was subtle but effective, often making people feel understood and respected, even if they disagreed with him. This combination of wisdom and empathy made him a trusted advisor, not just for his students, but for people of all walks of life.

The Influence on People in Positions of Power

It wasn't just the people in his immediate community who recognized Mr. Dhoriya's persuasive power; individuals in positions of authority also sought his guidance. One such instance occurred during election seasons, when the Returning Officers—those responsible for overseeing the electoral process would often approach Mr. Dhoriya for his insights. Whether the election was for a local legislative seat or the election of a Member of Parliament, his opinion carried weight. His deep understanding of human nature and his fair-minded approach made him a valuable asset to those who were responsible for ensuring the elections were fair and just.

In these politically charged environments, where opinions and allegiances could often be swayed by power, Mr. Dhoriya's advice was sought not because of any political standing or alliance, but because of his reputation for integrity. His advice, always measured and impartial, helped guide the process in ways that others couldn't. Whether it was advising on how to resolve conflicts that arose during the election process, or offering insights into the best ways to ensure that the elections were free from corruption, Mr. Dhoriya's words were always respected and often acted upon. This ability to influence people in positions of power was a testament to his understanding of human nature, his unshakable honesty, and his dedication to the greater good.

The Students Who Never Forgot

While Mr. Dhoriya's influence stretched beyond the walls of the classroom, it was in the classroom where his persuasive power truly shone. He didn't just teach English Literature; he imparted life lessons that his students would carry with them for the rest of their lives. His approach to teaching wasn't limited to books and theories; he understood that the heart of education lay in developing the character and mind of the student. His lessons were never confined to rote learning; they were about nurturing the soul.

Years after they graduated, many of his former students would return to express their gratitude. They often told him that his words, which seemed simple at the time, had a lasting impact on their lives. One former student recalled how Mr. Dhoriya had once told him, "The only thing that no one can take from you is your knowledge. The world may take your wealth, your home, but your education will stay with you forever. So, learn as much as you can." At the time, the student had dismissed it as just another piece of advice. But as the years went by, that message echoed in his mind whenever he faced challenges.

The greatest measure of Mr. Dhoriya's influence came when former students returned to share how his lessons had shaped their careers and relationships. Some became successful professionals, others made their way into politics, and many took on roles in their communities. Regardless of the paths they chose, they all had one thing in common: Mr. Dhoriya had made them believe in themselves and the power of education. His influence was woven into the fabric of their lives, and it was through his persuasive teaching style that they had been equipped with the tools to succeed.

The Case of the Troubled Student

Among the many students who came and went through Mr. Dhoriya's classroom, there was one who stood out—not for his academic success, but for his troubled nature. This student was notorious in the school for his constant misbehavior, his involvement in criminal activities, and his frequent altercations with both teachers and fellow students. He had been involved in over ten criminal cases, and his reputation was such that few would have expected anything positive to come from him.

Yet, there was something about Mr. Dhoriya that made this student listen. While other teachers might have resorted to harsh punishments or harsh words, Mr. Dhoriya's approach was different. He never raised his voice or resorted to violence. Instead, he calmly intervened, speaking with the student in private, understanding his struggles, and offering him guidance. It was a rare moment of understanding in an environment where this young man was often dismissed as trouble.The student, who would normally have been quick to lash out at anyone who tried to discipline him, found himself responding to Mr. Dhoriya's calm, steady presence. The words that Mr. Dhoriya spoke weren't always about discipline or correction—they were about the potential for change. "You have within you the ability to make a better choice, but only if you're willing to see things differently," he once told him. And that message, though simple, had a lasting effect.

Years later, when this student was preparing for one of the most important milestones of his life—his marriage—he did something unexpected. He chose to invite only one teacher from his past, someone who had never given up on him, even when others had. Mr. Dhoriya was the only teacher on the list. This act of respect was a powerful acknowledgment of the difference Mr. Dhoriya had made in his life. The troubled student had transformed, and a part of that transformation was due to the unshakeable belief that Mr. Dhoriya had in him, even when others had given up.

Overcoming Caste Barriers

Another remarkable aspect of Mr. Dhoriya's influence was his ability to transcend the social divisions that existed in his society. Coming from a marginalized Hindu caste, he could have easily been subjected to prejudice and discrimination. But Mr. Dhoriya's character was so strong, his integrity so evident, that such divisions never stood in his way. People respected him for what he stood for—not for the caste into which he was born.

In a town where caste divisions still played a significant role in how people interacted, Mr. Dhoriya was an anomaly. He was able to dine with the upper castes without hesitation or discomfort. Even the most rigid and conservative Hindus, who would have typically refused to share a meal with someone from his background, had no problem eating with him. His sincerity, his honesty, and his deep empathy for others made him a figure that people of all backgrounds could look up to. It wasn't his caste that defined him—it was his character, his work ethic, and his ability to connect with people on a human level.

His humility and sincerity broke down barriers that others could not even approach. People saw him for who he truly was: a man of respect, a man of learning, and a man who treated others with dignity, regardless of their background.

The Drunkard's Transformation

One of the most powerful examples of Mr. Dhoriya's persuasive abilities came in the form of a man in his neighborhood who had become a well-known drunkard. This man had squandered his health, his wealth, and his relationships due to his alcoholism. His physical health was rapidly deteriorating, and he was on the brink of self-destruction. Many in the community had written him off as a lost cause, but not Mr. Dhoriya.

He never judged the man for his behavior or his weaknesses. Instead, he took the time to listen to him. The man would often visit Mr. Dhoriya for a chat, seeking solace and counsel. It was in one of these conversations that the man, feeling completely hopeless, confided in Mr. Dhoriya that he was planning to end his life. He felt as though he had nothing left to live for, and the pain of his existence seemed too much to bear.

Mr. Dhoriya listened carefully, understanding the depth of the man's despair. But rather than offering simple words of comfort, he gave him something deeper: perspective. He told the man that taking his own life would be "anti-Hindu," as it went against the very teachings of his faith. He explained that life, with all its struggles, was part of the divine plan, and that even in his pain, the man had the power to choose his path forward. Mr. Dhoriya's calm, reasoned words struck a chord with the man, and he chose to abandon the idea of suicide. Instead, he began to seek help for his alcoholism and, slowly but surely, turned his life around.

This transformation was yet another testament to Mr. Dhoriya's persuasive power. It was not about preaching or forcing someone to change—it was about understanding their pain, offering them a different perspective, and helping them find the strength to make a better choice.

The Power of Persuasion

Mr. Dhoriya's life is a shining example of how persuasion, when used with integrity, empathy, and wisdom, can change lives. His influence was never about manipulating or controlling others; it was about making people see their own potential, their own worth, and the better choices they could make. Whether it was in the classroom, in his community, or in moments of personal crisis, Mr. Dhoriya's words were always rooted in a deep respect for others, and his persuasive ability became a force for positive change. Through his life, he showed that the greatest power lies in the ability to guide others with kindness, to inspire them with wisdom, and to convince them that they are capable of more than they ever imagined.

VI

Responsibility & Compassion

"The mediocre teacher tells. The good teacher explains. The superior teacher demonstrates. The great teacher inspires."
— William Arthur Ward

In the vast tapestry of human experience, where the threads of personal character and virtue intertwine to shape the lives of individuals, the legacy of Mr. Dhoriya stands as a testament to the enduring power of responsibility and kindness. These values, inherited from a lineage of remarkable ancestors and nurtured through the exigencies of a challenging early life, have remained steadfast beacons of guidance in Mr. Dhoriya's journey. His story, woven with perseverance, sacrifice, and an unwavering commitment to others, transcends the mundane concerns of everyday existence. Rather, it speaks to the nobler, often overlooked virtues that define the very essence of humanity.

Responsibility: The Cornerstone of Character

From the earliest stages of his life, Mr. Dhoriya was immersed in an environment that demanded a profound understanding of responsibility. Born into a large family of nine brothers—without a single sister—he was raised at a time when resources were not only scarce but fiercely contested. The burdens of existence were shared amongst all members of the household, and every day was a battle not merely for survival, but for cohesion, solidarity, and collective perseverance. In such a milieu, the notion of responsibility was not an abstract concept relegated to philosophical musings; it was a lived reality, a force that shaped every decision and every interaction.

As one of the eldest brothers, Mr. Dhoriya understood that the well-being of his siblings was, in part, entrusted to his care. His parents, tireless in their efforts to provide for their brood, had instilled in him a sense of duty that transcended personal comfort. Rather than shying away from this mantle, Mr. Dhoriya embraced it. The act of responsibility, in his eyes, was not merely a matter of fulfilling one's own obligations but extending that responsibility to the broader community. It was about cultivating a sense of shared purpose, a realization that individual actions reverberate within the collective fabric of society.

Thus, it was through this early immersion in responsibility that Mr. Dhoriya learned the delicate art of balancing his personal needs with those of others. Whether it was offering counsel to his younger brothers, assuming leadership in moments of crisis, or making personal sacrifices to alleviate the burdens of his parents, Mr. Dhoriya's sense of duty became a guiding light that illuminated every aspect of his life.

The Cell phone Habit: A Subtle Manifestation of Duty

In an age where technological advances have both connected and distanced us, Mr. Dhoriya's approach to communication offers a revealing glimpse into his character. It is said that a person's relationship with technology can often serve as a reflection of their broader life philosophy. Mr. Dhoriya, ever steadfast in his commitment to others, has cultivated a habit that speaks volumes about his sense of duty. Despite the frenetic pace of modern life, he has adopted a seemingly modest but profoundly significant practice: keeping his cellphone on at all times.

In an age where individuals—especially as they grow older—tend to curate their availability, choosing selectively when to engage with others, Mr. Dhoriya has refused to follow this trend. His cell phone, ever on and ever ready, serves as a conduit for his continuous availability. Day or night, he remains accessible to those in need of his counsel, guidance, or support. This seemingly trivial act is, in reality, an eloquent manifestation of his deep-rooted commitment to others. It requires not only a willingness to sacrifice personal comfort but also a quiet fortitude, a steady resolve to place the needs of others above one's own.

Whether it is an urgent call at 3 a.m. or a routine query during the day, Mr. Dhoriya answers with equal care, offering his time and attention with unwavering consistency. To him, responding to these calls is not an imposition but an extension of his lifelong dedication to service. He views the practice not as a mere obligation but as an opportunity to extend kindness and offer his help, no matter the hour. In this, we see how Mr. Dhoriya has redefined responsibility—not as a burden, but as a means of deepening human connection and fostering empathy.

A Man of His Word

In a time when promises are often treated as malleable, subject to the whims of convenience or circumstance, Mr. Dhoriya stands as a paragon of integrity. His word, once given, is as unyielding as the most ancient oaths. In both his personal and professional spheres, his reliability has become the very bedrock upon which his relationships are built. Whether dealing with family, colleagues, or students, Mr. Dhoriya has cultivated a reputation as a man who honors his commitments, irrespective of the challenges that may arise.

In a society that often embraces flexibility at the expense of commitment, Mr. Dhoriya's steadfast dedication to his promises is an anomaly, one that commands respect and admiration. His capacity to follow through with his word, no matter the external circumstances, has made him a beacon of trustworthiness. In an era marked by fleeting assurances, Mr. Dhoriya is a rare figure—one whose reliability forms the foundation of his relationships and his reputation. His life is a testament to the power of consistency and the quiet strength of a promise kept.

Kindness: The Heartbeat of Humanity

While responsibility may serve as the scaffolding upon which Mr. Dhoriya has built his life, it is his boundless kindness that breathes life into his interactions. His kindness, untainted by self-interest, extends far beyond the confines of family and friends. It touches the lives of acquaintances, strangers, and even those who may never repay him for his compassion. It is this openness of heart, this willingness to treat others with respect and empathy that truly sets Mr. Dhoriya apart.

One particularly poignant example of his kindness occurred during a misunderstanding with the parent of one of his students. Rather than responding with defensiveness or frustration, Mr. Dhoriya exhibited the grace of a seasoned diplomat. Calm and composed, he listened intently to the concerns of the parent, offering her the space to express her grievances without interruption. The situation, which could have easily spiralled into conflict, was instead transformed by Mr. Dhoriya's unwavering patience and empathy. His refusal to react impulsively allowed the tension to dissipate, fostering a space for understanding and reconciliation.

Even after the conversation had concluded, Mr. Dhoriya went one step further—he shared a cup of tea with the parent, signalling that his kindness was not merely performative but deeply ingrained in his daily life. In this moment, Mr. Dhoriya demonstrated that kindness is not merely a reactive emotion but an active choice, a decision to engage with the world with an open heart and an unwavering belief in the inherent goodness of others.

The Buddhist Way of Handling Conflict

Mr. Dhoriya's approach to handling difficult situations, particularly those involving conflict or criticism, is rooted in a philosophy that he has cultivated over many years. Deeply influenced by Buddhist teachings, he has internalized the principles of mindfulness, compassion, and non-reactivity. Rather than reacting impulsively to criticism or provocation, Mr. Dhoriya has learned to take a step back, assess the situation with clarity, and respond with a sense of calm equanimity.

This Buddhist-inspired philosophy has enabled Mr. Dhoriya to navigate the vicissitudes of life with a serenity that many find enviable. His refusal to engage in heated arguments or petty disputes is a manifestation of his commitment to maintaining inner peace. His calm demeanour, even in the face of unjust criticism, has earned him the respect of those who know him. His wife, however, sometimes finds his ability to remain unfazed frustrating, as she desires to defend him when others treat him poorly. Yet, Mr. Dhoriya remains unmoved, understanding that the actions of others are beyond his control, and that his response should always be guided by patience and empathy.

Conclusion: The Legacy of Responsibility and Kindness

In a time increasingly driven by haste, self-interest, and division, the life of Mr. Dhoriya offers a powerful reminder of the transformative potential of responsibility and kindness. Through his actions, he has demonstrated that responsibility is not simply the fulfilment of duties but a deep-seated commitment to others, to the community, and to the betterment of the world around us. His unwavering dedication to his word, his tireless availability to those in need, and his commitment to extending kindness at every opportunity make him a living embodiment of the values that can elevate human existence.

Mr. Dhoriya's life illustrates that the greatest leaders are not those who wield power or influence, but those who, with quiet resolve and a compassionate heart, inspire others through their actions. He has shown that the path to true fulfilment lies not in personal achievement or material success, but in the cultivation of responsibility, kindness, and a deep respect for the humanity of others. Through his example, Mr. Dhoriya has taught us all that it is not enough to live for oneself—we must live for others, always seeking to lift, support, and inspire those around us.

VII
Truth & Honour

In the rich tapestry of human existence, where the light of virtue often flickers amid the darkness of temptation, Mr. Dhoriya's life shines brightly as a paragon of integrity and honesty. These principles, which might seem distant and abstract to many, were not mere ideals for Mr. Dhoriya—they were the very foundation upon which he built both his personal character and professional career. In a climate where ethical compromises are often the easy route and the allure of shortcuts can cloud judgment, Mr. Dhoriya's steadfast commitment to truth, accountability, and fairness has remained unshaken. His life, therefore, offers us not only a mirror in which we can examine our own ethical convictions but also a beacon of inspiration that calls us to live by the same principles of integrity, regardless of the personal costs involved.

Living by Example: Consistency in Actions and Words

Mr. Dhoriya's belief in honesty was not confined to mere speeches or lofty declarations. For him, honesty was a way of life, an enduring principle that was to be consistently lived out through every action and interaction. The essence of integrity, as he demonstrated throughout his life, lay not in grand gestures, but in the small, seemingly inconsequential acts that often go unnoticed by others. Indeed, it is these very actions, carried out in the absence of an audience, that reveal the true measure of one's character.

A striking example of Mr. Dhoriya's consistency occurred in a simple yet profound moment. One day, he advised his nephew to endure the cold by using cold water for bathing, a recommendation made even more formidable by the chilly weather. Later that day, when Mr. Dhoriya himself faced the bracing discomfort of cold water, he refrained from taking the easy way out by heating his own water. Instead, he endured the same discomfort he had previously asked of his nephew, symbolizing his unyielding commitment to his own words.

This seemingly small act reveals a vital truth about integrity—it is not about seeking comfort or taking shortcuts when the stakes are low. Rather, integrity demands consistency, the alignment of one's actions with one's principles, regardless of convenience. Whether in the quiet of one's home or in the glare of public scrutiny, Mr. Dhoriya's actions mirrored his values. For him, honesty was not a situational virtue but a guiding constant that shaped his every decision. His willingness to make personal sacrifices in order to remain true to his word became a defining characteristic, showing that the essence of integrity lies in unwavering consistency, even when the path is difficult.

Facing Challenges with Patience and Dignity

As in every noble life, the path of honesty and integrity is not without its trials. Mr. Dhoriya's journey, too, was marked by moments where his commitment to these values was tested. One of the most notable instances of this occurred in the professional sphere, when a fellow teacher sought a transfer that Mr. Dhoriya had been granted. The teacher, frustrated by the perceived injustice, worked tirelessly to reverse the decision. Eventually, the transfer was rescinded, and Mr. Dhoriya's move was undone. But rather than reacting with bitterness or resentment, Mr. Dhoriya accepted the reversal with quiet grace and dignity.

In a situation where many would have sought to retaliate, engage in political manoeuvring, or harbour ill will, Mr. Dhoriya's response stood in stark contrast. He did not allow the situation to shake his resolve or cloud his judgment. Instead, he chose the path of patience, biding his time until the moment arrived when he would receive what he was due, but without bitterness or a desire for retribution. His quiet acceptance of an unfavourable outcome highlighted a profound aspect of integrity: it is not merely about standing firm in one's values when circumstances are in one's favour, but rather about maintaining one's principles even when the world around you seems unjust.

In this way, Mr. Dhoriya's life teaches us that true integrity is not measured by how one behaves during times of triumph but by how one conducts oneself in moments of adversity and perceived unfairness. His ability to withstand frustration without compromising his values serves as a powerful reminder that grace, patience, and dignity are integral to the exercise of integrity.

Selflessness and Responsibility: Putting the Greater Good First

One of the defining features of Mr. Dhoriya's character was his willingness to place the needs of others above his own. This selflessness was not a mere gesture or an occasional act of charity; rather, it was a core aspect of his personality, woven into the very fabric of his daily life. As a teacher, he understood the profound responsibility that came with his role, and he lived this responsibility with a deep sense of duty.

An exemplary instance of this selflessness occurred during an exam duty, when a colleague made a significant error that could have led to serious consequences for the entire team. Despite the fact that Mr. Dhoriya was not at fault, he chose to shoulder the responsibility for the mistake, standing by his colleague in their time of need. By doing so, Mr. Dhoriya took the moral high ground, accepting the potential consequences of the error without hesitation. This act of solidarity, borne out of a deep sense of responsibility, demonstrated that integrity involves not only doing what is right for oneself but also standing by others in their moments of failure or weakness.

Mr. Dhoriya's willingness to endure personal hardship for the sake of others speaks to a deeper understanding of integrity—that it is not a solitary pursuit, but one that is inextricably linked to the well-being of others. His actions exemplify the idea that true integrity is not about self-interest or self-preservation, but about putting the greater good first, even at great personal cost. Through this act of selflessness, Mr. Dhoriya reinforced his belief that integrity is not just about adhering to personal values, but about carrying the weight of collective responsibility.

Maintaining Professionalism and Accountability

In his professional life, Mr. Dhoriya embodied a standard of discipline, punctuality, and accountability that set him apart from many of his peers. His commitment to his duties, regardless of personal difficulties or external pressures, reflected his unwavering belief in the importance of responsibility. This was particularly evident in his approach to his work as a teacher. Over his 35 years of service, Mr. Dhoriya never wavered in his dedication to punctuality, to his students, and to the very values that had guided him throughout his life.

Perhaps one of the most telling moments of his professional integrity occurred during an inspection by an Education Inspector. While many would have sought to use their influence or connections to mitigate any unfavourable assessment, Mr. Dhoriya chose a different path. Despite his influential connections in the education system, he refused to seek external assistance or interfere with the process. Instead, he embraced the inspector's criticisms with humility and honesty, acknowledging his shortcomings without defensiveness. This rare display of professionalism demonstrated his commitment to growth and improvement, rather than seeking to manipulate outcomes or protect his reputation.

Through this, Mr. Dhoriya showed that true integrity lies not in seeking external validation or evading criticism, but in accepting responsibility and using feedback to improve. He remained steadfast in his belief that personal and professional growth is not achieved through manipulation or external influence but through an honest assessment of one's own actions and the willingness to learn from them.

A Life of Integrity

Mr. Dhoriya's life is a living testament to the timeless virtues of honesty and integrity. Whether in the quiet moments of daily life or in the face of significant professional and personal challenges, Mr. Dhoriya remained resolute in his commitment to these principles. His life serves as a poignant reminder that true character is not revealed in moments of triumph, but in how one handles adversity, embraces responsibility, and stays true to one's word.

In a time that often prioritizes expediency and shortcuts over ethical standards, Mr. Dhoriya's example stands as a beacon of hope. His unwavering adherence to the principles of honesty and integrity, even at personal cost, offers us a profound lesson: success is not measured by accolades, wealth, or influence, but by the purity of one's heart, the consistency of one's actions, and the steadfastness of one's principles. Mr. Dhoriya's life underscores that the highest achievement one can aspire to is to live a life of integrity, where one's actions consistently reflect one's values, and where the truth, no matter how inconvenient, is always upheld. Through his example, Mr. Dhoriya has shown us that integrity is not a mere choice, but a way of life, one that brings true fulfilment, peace, and lasting impact on the world around us.

VIII
Patience

"To lose patience is to lose the battle." **— Mahatma Gandhi**

Patience as an Immovable Force

Patience is often celebrated as a virtue in many cultures, but its true power and depth are understood by few. For Mr. Dhoriya, however, patience is not merely a virtue—it is an intrinsic strength, an unshakable cornerstone upon which the edifice of his entire life has been built. It has shaped his actions, guided his decisions, and fortified his resolve in the face of challenges that might have broken a lesser soul. In an age where instant gratification and rapid success are often pursued with fervor, patience remains a rare, almost forgotten quality, and in many ways, it has become undervalued. Patience, in its essence, is far more than the simple act of waiting; it is the capacity to endure with grace, to resist the urge for immediate results, and to trust that time will unveil the answers, the rewards, and the lessons that one needs. It is the quiet strength to hold one's ground amidst the turmoil of impatience, allowing life to unfold naturally, at its own pace. For Mr. Dhoriya, this has been more than a principle; it has been his guiding light, the very force that propelled him through the darkest days of his life. It was patience that carried him through hardship, sacrifice, and perseverance, and it was patience that taught him, and later imparted to others, that even the most difficult obstacles could be overcome.

This chapter will explore how patience has not only been a pillar of Mr. Dhoriya's personal journey but also a beacon of hope for his family, his students, and all who have had the privilege of knowing him. Through his life story, we come to understand that patience is not passive; it is a dynamic and active force, one that shapes our present and moulds our future.

The Tragic Loss of His Father: A Test of Enduring Patience

The painful and untimely death of Mr. Dhoriya's father at a young age could have devastated the spirit of any child. Such a loss, especially during the formative years of childhood, often leaves a gaping void that one can never quite fill. For many, the death of a father at such an early age would lead to bitterness, frustration, or a sense of hopelessness. But for Mr. Dhoriya, this traumatic event did not serve to break him, as it might have for others. Instead, it ignited within him a deep well of patience, one that would be cultivated and expanded throughout his life.

In the wake of his father's passing, Mr. Dhoriya found his anchor in his mother. A woman who had been thrust into the role of both mother and father, she became the unspoken pillar of the family, guiding them through the harsh realities of life. Though burdened with grief, she channelled her sorrow into strength, working tirelessly to ensure that her children never lacked the love and care that they needed. Her ability to persevere in the face of overwhelming grief was a silent lesson in patience that Mr. Dhoriya absorbed with deep reverence.

From his mother, Mr. Dhoriya learned that life's adversities do not define us; it is our response to them that shapes our future. Patience became his lifeline. Where others might have seen a series of insurmountable barriers, he learned to see them as challenges to be met with endurance, a testing of one's resilience. The death of his father, a heart-wrenching event, did not shatter Mr. Dhoriya's spirit; it set the stage for the development of a profound and enduring patience, a patience that would serve him throughout his life.

The 10th-Grade Board Exam: A Victory of Patience and Perseverance

In rural India, during the 1970s, passing the 10th-grade board exam was a significant milestone, one that was often out of reach for many children, particularly those from poor backgrounds. For children like Mr. Dhoriya, born into a family already struggling with the challenges of poverty, the prospect of finishing school was an improbable dream. The hardships he faced growing up could have easily deterred him from pursuing an education. However, Mr. Dhoriya's determination, coupled with an unwavering patience, allowed him to rise above his circumstances.

The 10th-grade board exam was a defining moment in his life, not just for the academic achievement it represented, but for the deeper, more profound lessons it imparted. Despite the financial limitations, the lack of resources, and the general reluctance of children from his village to pursue education, Mr. Dhoriya persevered. His success in this exam was not a result of overnight effort or last-minute cramming; rather, it was the fruit of steady, patient labour over the years.

For him, education was never just about passing exams. It was about hope—the hope of a future not limited by his birth circumstances. Through his patience, he gradually, almost imperceptibly, transcended the limitations of his environment. His triumph in passing the 10th-grade exam represented much more than a grade on paper; it was the first tangible sign that through consistent effort and patience, barriers could be broken and dreams could be realized.

Balancing Work and Study: Patience as a Means of Self-Improvement

Following his success in the 10th grade, Mr. Dhoriya did not allow himself the luxury of complacency. Instead, he sought out work in a local government office as a clerk, a position that brought both financial relief and a sense of stability. For most, this would have been the pinnacle of success—securing a stable job in a government institution was an achievement that many from his village would have considered sufficient. But Mr. Dhoriya, with his long-term vision, understood that this job was not his destination; it was simply a stepping stone.

In his early adulthood, Mr. Dhoriya embarked on the formidable journey of balancing his full-time job with his studies, enrolling in a Bachelor of Education (B.Ed.) program. This was a feat few could have accomplished, especially in a society where educational pursuits were often secondary to the need to earn a livelihood. His days were long, filled with the gruelling demands of both work and study, and his sacrifices were immense. But Mr. Dhoriya's belief in the power of patience allowed him to endure these hardships.

Rather than becoming frustrated with the seemingly endless cycle of work and study, Mr. Dhoriya approached each day with patience and purpose. He knew that the road to success would not be swift, but he trusted that every effort would eventually bear fruit. The years he spent balancing work and study were difficult, yet they were also foundational, for they taught him that success does not come in a rush, but through gradual, deliberate progress.

Teaching Patience: The Role of an Educator

As Mr. Dhoriya transitioned from being a student to becoming a teacher, his understanding of patience evolved even further. He had now experienced firsthand the challenges of balancing work, study, and family responsibilities, and he knew that his students, too, would face their own struggles. In the classroom, patience became not only a virtue but a teaching philosophy. He understood that each student's journey was unique, and that success could not always be measured by immediate results or rapid progress.

For Mr. Dhoriya, teaching was about far more than simply imparting knowledge. It was about instilling values in his students—values of persistence, resilience, and, above all, patience. He encouraged them to embrace their challenges, to accept their failures as part of their growth process, and to trust that success would come if they remained steadfast in their efforts. His own life was a testament to this truth, and his students found inspiration not only in his lessons but also in his example.

Mr. Dhoriya taught his students that setbacks were not failures to be feared, but opportunities for growth. He showed them that the journey toward success was often slow, but it was always steady. His influence extended beyond textbooks and exams; he became a mentor, a guide, and a symbol of the transformative power of patience.

Family Challenges: Nurturing Patience in His Sons

One of the greatest tests of Mr. Dhoriya's patience came in the form of his own children. As a father, he understood the importance of offering support and encouragement in the face of setbacks. His elder son, despite his best efforts, failed his 12th-grade science exams. For many parents, this might have been a source of anger or disappointment, but not for Mr. Dhoriya. Instead, he offered words of wisdom, patience, and support, encouraging his son to view failure as part of the larger journey toward success.

Over time, his son persevered, finding his path and eventually becoming an Assistant Professor in a Government Grant-in-Aided College. This was a victory not just for his son, but for Mr. Dhoriya's belief in the power of patience and encouragement. It was a moment that proved, once again, that patience—when coupled with love and understanding—can lead to incredible transformations.

Similarly, Mr. Dhoriya's younger son faced his own set of challenges. Struggling with indecision about his career, he often felt lost, unsure of his direction. However, Mr. Dhoriya's patience never faltered. He allowed his son the time and space to explore his options without the pressure to meet conventional expectations. Eventually, his son found his calling, achieving success on his own terms. Again, it was Mr. Dhoriya's patient guidance that played a crucial role in shaping his son's journey.

Patience in Relationships: A Harmonious Partnership with His Wife

In his relationship with his wife, Mr. Dhoriya exhibited the same quiet patience that had defined his approach to life. Though she was illiterate, he never saw her as lesser or inadequate. He treated her with the utmost respect, valuing her strength and resilience in ways that transcended societal norms. Their marriage, built on mutual understanding and respect, was a partnership forged in patience.

Patience, in their relationship, meant growing together, learning together, and supporting each other's potential. It was an understanding that love, too, required time to bloom and evolve. Just as Mr. Dhoriya had patiently nurtured his own growth, so too did he offer the same patience and space for his wife to flourish in her own way.

The Indomitable Power of Patience

Mr. Dhoriya's life is a living testament to the quiet but formidable power of patience. From personal loss to professional triumph, from family struggles to educational achievements, his journey underscores the idea that true success is not defined by immediate results, but by a steady, patient pursuit of one's goals. In a time that often values speed, instant success, and quick gratification, Mr. Dhoriya's story serves as a powerful reminder that real strength lies not in hurrying, but in taking the time to grow, learn, and endure. His life exemplifies the profound truth that with patience, one can overcome any obstacle, navigate through any hardship, and emerge victorious—not just in terms of external accomplishments, but in the richness of personal growth, the depth of relationships, and the meaningful impact on others' lives. Through patience, we find not just success but fulfilment, purpose, and peace.

IX
Non-Indulgence

"You will never have a greater or lesser dominion than that over yourself... the height of a man's success is gauged by his self-mastery; the depth of his failure by his self-abandonment...and this is the law of eternal justice. He who cannot establish dominion over himself will have no dominion over others."
— Leonardo Da Vinci

In an age defined by excess, where indulgence is often paraded as a symbol of success, and where material gain is seen as the ultimate achievement, Mr. Dhoriya stands in stark contrast. His life is not a manifestation of what he consumes, but rather a reflection of what he resists. Mr. Dhoriya embodies the timeless philosophy that true luxury lies not in the acquisition of material possessions, nor in the overindulgence of sensory pleasures, but in the wisdom of moderation. This restraint, far from being a sign of deprivation, is a profound source of strength, self-mastery, and peace.

In an environment where convenience, excess, and immediate gratification often define success, Mr. Dhoriya has chosen a path of conscious restraint—a path that champions the art of living wisely and purposefully, without succumbing to the whims of indulgence. His life's example calls for introspection and offers a model for those seeking a more meaningful existence, grounded in simplicity, discipline, and the subtle luxury of moderation.

Below, we explore the philosophy of non-indulgence that has guided Mr. Dhoriya throughout his life, touching upon the multifaceted ways in which restraint and self-discipline have shaped his personal growth, relationships, and overall outlook on life.

A Conscious Lifestyle

At the core of Mr. Dhoriya's philosophy is his conscious approach to living—a deliberate and mindful way of interacting with the world. In a society that often glorifies the pursuit of excess, Mr. Dhoriya has adopted a life of simplicity and intentionality. Every action he takes, every decision he makes, and every interaction he engages in is governed by the principle of moderation. His life is a living testament to the idea that one does not need to indulge in the fleeting pleasures of material wealth or sensory excess to experience joy, contentment, and fulfilment.

Mr. Dhoriya's motto—"Live moderately, live fully"—resonates deeply in every area of his existence. His restraint is not a result of austerity or deprivation, but rather a commitment to living intentionally, with clarity and purpose. To Mr. Dhoriya, true success does not lie in the accumulation of possessions or in the consumption of worldly pleasures; it lies in mastering oneself, in resisting the temptations that often lead to a distracted, unfulfilling life.

Beyond Abstinence

For Mr. Dhoriya, non-indulgence is not about abstinence for its own sake—it is about finding balance and harmony in every aspect of his life. While many associate indulgence with freedom, he knows that true freedom arises from self-control. He believes that the ability to resist the pull of excessive desires is one of the highest forms of personal liberation. By choosing moderation, Mr. Dhoriya has discovered a life of inner peace and a deep sense of contentment, unburdened by the constant pursuit of more. In his world, less is more, and simplicity is the ultimate form of richness.

A Rare Stance

In a society where alcohol is often viewed as a social lubricant, Mr. Dhoriya's decision to abstain from drinking is a notable and rare stance. In an era where social gatherings are often synonymous with drinking, he remains unmoved by the pressures to conform. His choice to remain sober is not an act of judgment or superiority but a reflection of his personal commitment to maintaining control over his actions and desires. For Mr. Dhoriya, alcohol does not serve a purpose beyond temporary enjoyment—it is not something he needs to partake in to feel connected to others.

His friends and colleagues may enjoy a drink together, but Mr. Dhoriya's presence remains unaffected. He will join in conversations, share laughter, and partake in the camaraderie of the moment, but his drink is always a modest one, often water or a soft drink. His decision to abstain from alcohol is not an expression of disdain for others, but rather a commitment to his own principles, a reminder that he does not need external validation to find peace within himself.

Social Harmony, Not Conformity

What makes Mr. Dhoriya's stance truly remarkable is his ability to maintain social harmony without sacrificing his own values. At social gatherings where alcohol flows freely, Mr. Dhoriya's composure never wavers. He does not feel the need to justify his choice, nor does he seek to impose it on others. His decision to drink water or soda, while everyone around him raises their glasses, is a quiet act of self-discipline and a gentle reminder that true social connection does not require indulgence in excess.

Mr. Dhoriya's example is a model of maturity and self-assurance. His restraint highlights the strength of his willpower and his unwavering sense of self. In an atmosphere that often associates drinking with fun and freedom, Mr. Dhoriya shows that one can enjoy life, socialize, and build meaningful connections without resorting to indulgence. His path is a quiet rebellion against the notion that one must partake in excess to feel a sense of belonging.

Eating with Grace and Moderation

In a culture where eating has often become a mindless, indulgent activity, Mr. Dhoriya's approach to food stands as a testament to his discipline and mindfulness. Observing him as he eats is an experience in itself—one that speaks to the profound relationship he has with food. For Mr. Dhoriya, eating is not about satisfying cravings or indulgent pleasures; it is about nourishment. Each meal is a conscious act, a ritual that nurtures both body and mind. He eats slowly, savoring every bite, not because the food is indulgent, but because it is necessary for his well-being and vitality.

He is not in a hurry to finish his meal, nor does he overeat, regardless of how tempting the food may be. For Mr. Dhoriya, eating is a form of self-care, a discipline that ensures he is fuelling his body with the right amount of nutrition without falling into the trap of excess. He follows the simple yet profound rule of leaving his stomach 25% empty, a practice that ensures his body remains light and energized, never burdened by the weight of overeating.

Eating to Live, Not Living to Eat

This is perhaps one of the most striking demonstrations of Mr. Dhoriya's non-indulgent philosophy. He embodies the age-old wisdom that "man must not live to eat, but eat to live." His relationship with food is one of respect and balance, not indulgence. While many in today's world eat to satisfy their emotional needs or to indulge in the pleasures of taste, Mr. Dhoriya eats with purpose and clarity. Each meal is a means to sustain his body, enabling him to carry out the important work and responsibilities that life presents.

By practicing mindful consumption, Mr. Dhoriya avoids the trap of overindulgence that often characterizes the modern world. He is a living example of how one can remain healthy, content, and fulfilled without giving in to the temptation to overconsume. His restraint in eating is a reflection of his broader philosophy of life—one that emphasizes balance, moderation, and mindfulness in every area of existence.

The Dangers of Excess

Mr. Dhoriya's commitment to non-indulgence is deeply rooted in his understanding of the dangers that excess can bring. Whether it's food, drink, or material possessions, he has seen firsthand the destructive power of overindulgence. He understands that the more one consumes, the more one is enslaved by desire, leading to a cycle of dissatisfaction, emptiness, and eventual self-destruction.

Through his own experiences, Mr. Dhoriya has learned that true fulfilment does not lie in the acquisition of more but in the wisdom of knowing when enough is enough. By resisting the temptations of excess, he has been able to maintain a sense of peace and contentment that cannot be achieved through indulgence. In a society that often promotes the idea that more is better, Mr. Dhoriya stands as a quiet critic of this mindset, advocating instead for the virtues of restraint, simplicity, and self-mastery.

The Virtue of Abstinence

For Mr. Dhoriya, abstinence is not about denying oneself joy or pleasure; rather, it is about understanding that true happiness comes not from indulgence, but from inner peace and balance. His abstinence from excess is a form of self-love, a recognition that he is worthy of the peace that comes from living in moderation. By choosing not to indulge in the transient pleasures of the world, Mr. Dhoriya has cultivated a sense of richness that cannot be measured in material wealth. His restraint is a symbol of his inner strength, his ability to say no to what is unnecessary, and his commitment to living with purpose and clarity.

Respect for Boundaries

One of the most beautiful aspects of Mr. Dhoriya's character is the respect he shows for the boundaries of others. He understands that relationships, whether familial, social, or professional, must be built on a foundation of mutual respect and consideration. Before meeting anyone, Mr. Dhoriya always ensures that the other person is genuinely available to engage with him. This small but significant act demonstrates his understanding of the importance of time and space, not just for himself, but for others as well.

By being considerate of others' boundaries, Mr. Dhoriya creates an environment of mutual respect, where interactions are meaningful and free from the pressure to conform to social expectations. This respectful approach fosters deeper, more genuine connections, allowing him to build relationships based on trust, understanding, and empathy.

Family First

Mr. Dhoriya's love for his family is quiet but unwavering. He does not seek to demonstrate his love through extravagant gestures or public displays of affection. Instead, he shows his love through his actions—through his constant care for their well-being, his support during difficult times, and his unwavering commitment to being a reliable presence in their lives. His love is not driven by the need for validation but by a deep sense of duty and responsibility.

For Mr. Dhoriya, the most powerful form of love is not in grand declarations but in the small, everyday acts that demonstrate care, consideration, and thoughtfulness. He understands that love is not about indulgence or seeking personal gratification but about selfless giving, sharing, and being present for others in their moments of need.

The Beauty of Simplicity

In his relationships, Mr. Dhoriya seeks simplicity. He does not indulge in the extravagance or complexity that often define modern relationships. Instead, he values the small, everyday moments of connection—whether it's a quiet conversation, a gesture of kindness, or simply being there for someone when they need support. For Mr. Dhoriya, the true beauty of a relationship lies not in its grandeur but in its authenticity and simplicity.

A Life of Luxury in Restraint

In an environment where luxury is often equated with excess—luxury cars, large homes, expensive clothes—Mr. Dhoriya has discovered that the truest form of luxury lies in restraint. He has chosen a life free from the distractions of overconsumption, finding joy and fulfillment not in the accumulation of things but in the richness of self-mastery and inner peace. His lifestyle may not boast of material wealth, but it exudes a rare form of luxury—a luxury of the spirit, one that is not available through indulgence or excess.

A Timeless Legacy

Mr. Dhoriya's commitment to living a non-indulgent life may not result in grand public displays of wealth or success, but it has created a legacy that is far more enduring and meaningful. His life serves as a reminder that true richness is not found in what one possesses, but in what one is able to resist—the distractions, temptations, and excesses that pull us away from what truly matters.

The Power of Restraint

In an era where indulgence is often celebrated as the pinnacle of human experience, Mr. Dhoriya's life stands as a rare example of the transformative power of restraint. His journey demonstrates that true success is not measured by what one acquires or consumes, but by the wisdom to live simply, intentionally, and with purpose. By embracing moderation and self-discipline, Mr. Dhoriya has created a life that is rich not in material possessions, but in clarity, peace, and fulfilment. Through his example, we learn that true luxury lies in living wisely and moderately, with meaning, connection, and inner peace.

X
Morality

"*Morality is not the doctrine of how we may make ourselves happy, but how we may make ourselves worthy of happiness.*"
—Immanuel Kant

In a society often swayed by the tides of materialism, instant gratification, and ethical compromises, Mr. Dhoriya's life stands as an unwavering testament to the power of moral integrity. Amidst a world increasingly focused on shortcuts and momentary indulgences, few have held fast to their moral principles with such consistency and clarity as Mr. Dhoriya. His journey, one of tireless dedication and righteous action, was defined not just by external achievements but by an internal compass—an unshakable adherence to values that guided his every decision and action.

For Mr. Dhoriya, morality was not a passive doctrine or a mere set of guidelines to follow when convenient. It was the very bedrock upon which he built his relationships, his career, and his legacy. It was a guiding force that directed him through both the trials of personal struggle and the temptations that life inevitably presented. His commitment to this unwavering moral code, drawn from a deep-rooted sense of personal responsibility and ethical duty, became the cornerstone of his character.

A Life Anchored in Faithfulness

Morality, in its truest form, manifests through the quiet actions and decisions we make each day, and for Mr. Dhoriya, this was a reality that he lived by in every aspect of his existence. His moral integrity was not confined to abstract theories or words; it was reflected in his actions, grounded firmly in the day-to-day choices he made. Where temptation lurks at every corner and ethical lapses are often met with indifference or even encouragement, Mr. Dhoriya's steadfastness stood out as a beacon of righteousness.

His dedication to moral uprightness wasn't something he preached from a distance. Mr. Dhoriya was deeply aware of the example he set for others, especially the younger generation who looked up to him as a teacher and mentor. As someone who understood the challenges posed by a world where ethical boundaries are often blurred, he chose to stand firm, to remain unwavering in his commitment to fidelity, truthfulness, and honesty.

This personal commitment extended beyond his own life and into the lives of those around him. Mr. Dhoriya believed in not just teaching his students academic subjects but in guiding them toward a stronger moral foundation. As a teacher, he understood the profound influence his actions and words would have on his students. He considered it his sacred duty to ensure that, in addition to learning from textbooks, his students would also learn valuable life lessons about integrity, responsibility, and the importance of adhering to an ethical code.

The Role of Culture and Tradition in Shaping Morality

Mr. Dhoriya's moral framework was deeply shaped by the timeless values embedded in Indian culture and tradition. Indian spiritual and philosophical teachings, grounded in principles of dharma (righteousness) and satya (truth), became the very essence of his moral outlook. These age-old traditions, which revered values such as fidelity, humility, and self-restraint, offered Mr. Dhoriya a robust blueprint for living a life of integrity.

He often spoke of how the fabric of Indian society had historically woven moral values into the very structure of daily life, emphasizing the importance of a faithful marriage and the sanctity of familial bonds. For Mr. Dhoriya, this cultural inheritance was not just a social norm; it was a moral guideline that ensured a strong, harmonious society. By adhering to these values, he believed one could achieve not just individual fulfilment but also contribute to the overall well-being of the community.

This reverence for tradition and moral structure was reflected in his approach to personal relationships. Mr. Dhoriya's commitment to marital fidelity was a key element of his character. He viewed it not as a mere societal expectation but as a sacred moral obligation. His dedication to maintaining trust and respect within his family was a direct manifestation of his belief in the strength that comes from personal integrity.

As a teacher, Mr. Dhoriya would often remind his students that the decisions they made in their personal lives, particularly in their relationships, were not just about their own happiness but about the kind of people they would become. He would often say, "The decisions you make today will shape who you become tomorrow. And there is no greater wealth than the strength of a character built on trust and respect." These words were more than just lessons; they were reflections of Mr. Dhoriya's own unwavering moral compass.

The Struggles of a Young Teacher in a Morally Challenging Environment

When Mr. Dhoriya first began his teaching career, he was stationed in a small village that presented him with an environment that could easily have led him astray. The village, he recalled, was a place where many young people had lost their way, succumbing to the temptations of fleeting pleasures. There was a prevailing culture of indulgence, where instant gratification seemed to be the norm and the deeper values of life were often sidelined.

At 27 years old, newly appointed as a teacher, Mr. Dhoriya faced the dual challenge of adapting to this morally ambiguous environment while remaining true to the values he held so dear. The pressures of living in such a setting were intense, and it would have been easy to get swept away by the current of popular behaviour, but Mr. Dhoriya did not falter. He recognized that his primary mission was not just to educate young minds but to serve as a moral example for them.

In a place where the moral fabric seemed to have worn thin, where indulgence in fleeting pleasures was the norm, Mr. Dhoriya's steadfastness became even more apparent. Despite the temptations that surrounded him, he remained unwavering in his commitment to his personal ethics. His dedication to teaching wasn't just about academics—it was about nurturing character and instilling values that would last a lifetime. As he taught his students about math, literature, or history, he would also guide them on the importance of maintaining one's moral compass, regardless of external pressures.

He believed that true success in life wasn't measured by achievements that were momentary or external but by the integrity one maintained in the face of life's inevitable challenges. His life was proof of the strength one could derive from unwavering principles, and he shared this belief with his students through personal anecdotes and life lessons.

The Ripple Effect of Morality

As the years went by, the impact of Mr. Dhoriya's moral teachings began to reverberate far beyond the walls of his classroom. His influence reached into the homes of his students and into the fabric of the community. Many of those who had been initially swayed by the allure of transient pleasures began to reflect on their choices, reconsidering the long-term consequences of their actions. Mr. Dhoriya's guidance had planted the seed of self-reflection and moral clarity, which began to grow in the hearts of his students.

Over time, many of Mr. Dhoriya's students would return to him—not just to thank him for his academic guidance but to express their gratitude for the moral direction he had provided. They would share how his teachings had shaped their decisions, not just in terms of career choices but in their relationships, their personal lives, and their broader approach to life's challenges. For many, Mr. Dhoriya had shown them that the most important things in life were not the fleeting pleasures of the moment but the enduring values that guided one's actions and decisions.

In those moments, when his former students expressed their gratitude, Mr. Dhoriya would reflect on his journey. His life wasn't one of grand accolades or fleeting success. It was a quiet, steadfast journey built on principles that transcended time and circumstance. The true measure of his success wasn't in personal fame or recognition but in the lasting legacy he left in the hearts of others—one rooted in morality, integrity, and selflessness.

Mr. Dhoriya's life is a shining example of the power of morality in action. Where ethical lines are often blurred and indulgence is frequently celebrated, he stood as a beacon of unwavering commitment to righteousness. His dedication to living a life of integrity, not for the sake of personal gain but for the betterment of others, offers a profound lesson in how morality, when practiced in its truest sense, can transform not just the individual but the world around them.

In a society that often prizes material success and immediate gratification, Mr. Dhoriya's life serves as a reminder that the true wealth one can possess is not of monetary value but the strength of one's character. His legacy will endure long after his time, not because of his academic achievements or professional accomplishments, but because of the way he lived—guided by a moral compass that was unwavering, steady, and always directed toward the highest ideals of integrity and righteousness.

Through his teachings, his relationships, and his quiet but firm adherence to his principles, Mr. Dhoriya exemplified the profound impact that a life of moral action can have. In the end, it is not the external rewards we seek that define our lives but the strength with which we stand by what is right, regardless of the temptations and challenges that come our way.

XI

Communication

"Half the world is composed of people who have something to say and can't, and the other half who have nothing to say and keep on saying it." – Robert Frost

Communication, when executed well, serves as the bridge between individuals, fostering understanding, connection, and meaningful interaction. This fundamental human tool is often taken for granted, yet it is one of the most powerful vehicles for influence, growth, and harmony. In the case of Mr. Dhoriya, communication became not just a daily skill, but the lifeblood of his personal and professional relationships. For him, communication was not merely about transmitting information—it was about building trust, offering guidance, and ensuring that his words resonated with clarity, purpose, and empathy.

The following sections delve deeper into Mr. Dhoriya's unique approach to communication, illustrating how it shaped his career, family life, and legacy. Through his remarkable skill as both a listener and a speaker, he touched the lives of countless individuals, empowering them to make better decisions, foster deeper relationships, and contribute positively to their communities.

The Bedrock of Effective Teaching

At the heart of every great teacher is the ability to communicate effectively. In Mr. Dhoriya's case, this communication is built upon two vital attributes: an exceptional ear to listen and a well-practiced tongue to speak. These tools, though seemingly simple, are the essence of great teaching. A teacher can only truly connect with their students and peers when they actively listen and then respond with thoughtfulness, clarity, and purpose. For Mr. Dhoriya, communication became more than a skill; it was a moral duty and a responsibility to those who entrusted him with their time and their questions.

The Power of Listening

Mr. Dhoriya's capacity to listen attentively was extraordinary. For him, listening was never a passive activity. He believed that truly hearing someone meant understanding not only their words but also the emotions, insecurities, and thoughts that lay beneath the surface. This skill enabled him to form deeper connections with his students and others in his community. Whether it was a student seeking guidance on academic matters, a colleague sharing personal struggles, or a friend asking for advice, Mr. Dhoriya's first instinct was always to listen—not just to hear, but to understand.

He would often spend hours in quiet conversation, never rushing to offer advice, but allowing the other person to speak freely and express themselves fully. This approach of active listening made people feel heard and valued, and in turn, they were more likely to trust his insights and consider his advice with an open heart.

Speaking with Purpose and Clarity

Equally important was Mr. Dhoriya's ability to speak—an art he had refined over the years. His words were never rushed or superfluous; they were measured, deliberate, and always relevant to the moment. Mr. Dhoriya's speech had the power to resonate, and his conversations were a blend of wisdom, empathy, and clarity. He never spoke for the sake of speaking. His words were tools to foster understanding, resolve confusion, and inspire action.

Whether in the classroom or during personal discussions, Mr. Dhoriya's communication was always purposeful. His teachings were clear, his advice practical, and his manner humble. Students appreciated his ability to break down complex ideas and present them in digestible, relatable ways. Mr. Dhoriya understood that great communication required not just speaking but speaking with the right intention—intending to uplift, clarify, and empower.

Breaking Barriers of Distance and Time

In today's world, time constraints and personal distractions often lead people to avoid deep, meaningful conversations. However, Mr. Dhoriya has always made himself available for anyone in need of guidance, regardless of the time or nature of the problem. His open-door policy, a practice he embraced for decades, was not motivated by obligation but by genuine care and compassion. Whether it was a late-night phone call or a sudden visit in the middle of the day, Mr. Dhoriya would always make time for those who sought him out.

This accessibility was not a reflection of his duty as a teacher but an intrinsic part of his character. He understood that people often needed someone to listen, someone who could help them navigate their thoughts, fears, and dilemmas. By making himself accessible, Mr. Dhoriya created a safe space for others to express their worries, knowing that they would be met with empathy and understanding. In a time that often demands quick solutions or dismissive responses, Mr. Dhoriya's unwavering availability made him a trusted confidant to many.

Building Trust through Accessibility

Trust is the foundation of all meaningful relationships, and Mr. Dhoriya knew that being approachable was key to establishing that trust. Over the years, he earned a reputation for being someone who listened without judgment, offered guidance without preaching, and who always provided a helping hand when needed. People came to him not just for advice but for reassurance and support. They knew that his advice came from a place of understanding and experience and that he genuinely wanted the best for them.

Through his actions, Mr. Dhoriya demonstrated that communication is not just about speaking; it's about being present, offering emotional support, and establishing rapport. His kindness and patience created a network of people who felt valued and supported by him. As a result, he became a central figure in his community, someone whose counsel was sought and cherished by many.

Solving Complex Problems with Empathy

One of the most striking examples of Mr. Dhoriya's ability to use communication to guide others came when a young couple visited him, uncertain whether the wife should accept a promising job offer. The situation was delicate—her career advancement was tempting, but it would require significant changes to their family dynamics. She felt torn between her professional aspirations and the needs of her family. Mr. Dhoriya, ever the empathetic listener, allowed them to express their concerns fully before offering any advice.

Rather than giving immediate solutions, he asked questions that encouraged the wife to examine her own feelings and motivations. He gently prodded her to reflect on her values, her priorities, and how the decision would align with her vision for the future. This process of self-reflection empowered her to make a decision that felt right for her—one that balanced her professional aspirations with her family's needs.

The Art of Speaking at the Right Moment

Mr. Dhoriya understood that sometimes, the most powerful communication is found not in the words spoken, but in the pauses and silences that allow for reflection. He knew that his role was not to solve problems for others but to create an environment in which individuals could arrive at their own answers. This ability to speak at the right moment, knowing when to offer advice and when to remain silent, was a hallmark of his wisdom.

In a setting where everyone seems eager to offer opinions and solutions, Mr. Dhoriya's calm and measured approach to communication stood out. He recognized that some decisions require time, contemplation, and a deep understanding of one's own needs and desires. By allowing people to reflect, he empowered them to take ownership of their choices and decisions, ultimately leading to more fulfilling outcomes.

Breaking the Boundaries of Education and Literacy

Communication is not just essential in professional settings; it is equally vital in personal relationships. Mr. Dhoriya's communication within his family reflected his belief in mutual respect and understanding. Despite his wife's illiteracy, he never treated her as someone incapable of making informed decisions. In fact, he actively sought her input on important matters, recognizing that her experiences and perspectives were invaluable.

Mr. Dhoriya's approach was grounded in the belief that communication transcends formal education. True communication, for him, was about respect, inclusion, and understanding. He never allowed the fact that his wife was illiterate to diminish her voice or role in their shared life. This inclusive approach fostered a deeper sense of partnership, where both he and his wife could make decisions together as equals.

Parenting with Empathy

Mr. Dhoriya's communication with his son further demonstrated his commitment to empathy and understanding. When his son faced failure in his board exams, rather than resorting to frustration or harsh reprimands, Mr. Dhoriya communicated with patience and clarity. He took the time to understand his son's struggles and, instead of pushing him into a field he was not interested in, gently encouraged him to pursue the arts—a decision that ultimately allowed his son to flourish.

This approach is a powerful example of how communication within a family can empower individuals to grow, learn, and make choices that align with their passions and abilities. By listening attentively to his son's struggles and guiding him with empathy, Mr. Dhoriya reinforced the importance of communication not just as a tool for conveying information, but as a means of fostering trust, understanding, and personal growth.

Owning Mistakes with Honesty

Integrity in communication is crucial, and Mr. Dhoriya was a living testament to this principle. When faced with a mistake during his duties as an exam supervisor, rather than hiding the error or deflecting blame, he openly communicated the issue to his superior. He acknowledged the mistake as a human error, not a deliberate act of negligence. This honesty not only resolved the immediate issue but also strengthened his reputation as a trustworthy and responsible individual.

The Role of Integrity in Building Trust

Mr. Dhoriya's unwavering commitment to honesty and transparency was foundational to the trust he built over the years. His open communication, even in difficult situations, created an atmosphere of respect and reliability. People knew they could rely on him to be forthcoming with information, regardless of the outcome.

By consistently communicating with integrity, Mr. Dhoriya set a standard for others to follow. His actions demonstrated that effective communication is rooted not just in words, but in the truth and sincerity behind those words. This transparency empowered others to communicate more openly themselves, fostering an environment of mutual respect and understanding.

The Enduring Legacy of Communication

Mr. Dhoriya's remarkable ability to communicate effectively is the cornerstone of his success, both as a teacher and as a person. His life exemplifies how powerful communication can be in transforming not only the lives of those around him but also the very fabric of the communities he touches. Through active listening, thoughtful speech, empathy, transparency, and integrity, he has established himself as a beacon of guidance for many, not merely in academic matters but in all aspects of life.

His legacy is one of open dialogue, mutual respect, and an unwavering commitment to using the power of communication to uplift and empower others.

Through Mr. Dhoriya's actions, we learn that communication is not just a tool—it is an art, an essential thread that weaves the fabric of relationships, understanding, and shared humanity. His life reminds us that the greatest communicators are not those who speak the loudest or most frequently, but those who know when to listen, when to speak, and when to remain silent—offering words that heal, guide, and inspire.

XII
Guilelessness

The True Meaning of Guilelessness: A Deliberate Choice of Integrity

In an era where manipulation, strategy, and calculated moves are often seen as keys to success, Mr. Dhoriya's life provides a profound lesson in the beauty and strength of guilelessness. Guilelessness, in its essence, is not about being naive or weak. It is about choosing to live with authenticity and integrity, rejecting the need for deception, and choosing honesty as a way of life. Mr. Dhoriya's life is a shining example of how living with guilelessness can be a conscious, powerful decision—a life marked by moral clarity, truth, and unwavering adherence to values, even in the face of a world that often thrives on manipulation.

At its core, guilelessness is an intentional decision to refuse to engage in manipulation, dishonesty, or pretension. It means staying true to oneself and one's principles, regardless of external pressures. In a society where many people often wear masks to navigate their social and professional lives—adapting their behaviours, thoughts, and words to meet the expectations of others—Mr. Dhoriya has steadfastly resisted this approach. Instead, he has chosen to be true to himself in every circumstance, a rare and remarkable choice that has shaped his character.

Guilelessness is a refusal to compromise one's values for the sake of success, social acceptance, or personal gain. It does not mean ignoring the complexities of life or the challenges presented by others who might manipulate or deceive. Rather, it is a deliberate decision to stay true to one's principles and to remain open, honest, and authentic. Mr. Dhoriya's commitment to this way of life is both revolutionary and deeply humbling. While others often seek power, influence, or material wealth through calculated moves, Mr. Dhoriya remains steadfast in his belief that authenticity and integrity are the truest forms of wealth. These virtues, though sometimes undervalued by society, are the foundations of lasting peace, happiness, and fulfilment.

By living a life of guilelessness, Mr. Dhoriya has found inner peace—something that is increasingly rare in a world full of superficiality and hidden agendas. While many may wear masks to conceal their true selves in order to climb the social or professional ladder, Mr. Dhoriya's journey has been one of truth, openness, and consistency. His example serves as a poignant reminder that true success is measured not by the number of accolades we accumulate but by how true we remain to our own hearts. And in a world where deception is often rewarded, Mr. Dhoriya's choice to remain authentic is nothing short of revolutionary.

The Betrayal of a Friend: The Test of Character

The true test of character often comes not in times of triumph or comfort, but in moments of adversity and betrayal. How does one respond when faced with deceit, especially from someone they trusted deeply? For Mr. Dhoriya, this challenge arrived early in his career when he found himself betrayed by a close friend and colleague, a man with whom he had shared not only professional respect but also a bond of camaraderie. This colleague was from the same community and worked alongside Mr. Dhoriya in the same educational institution. Their relationship was grounded in mutual admiration and the belief that they shared similar principles and goals.

However, as is often the case in professional environments, ambition, and career progression bring with them moments of vulnerability and moral challenges. Teachers in their region were expected to undergo transfers, which were tied to the potential for higher salaries and better career prospects. This system, which was supposed to be based on merit and seniority, often revealed the inherent flaws of bureaucracy—where manipulation could take precedence over fairness. It was within this environment that Mr. Dhoriya's colleague saw an opportunity to use the system for his own advantage.

Though this colleague was not next in line for the transfer, he somehow managed to convince the District Education Officer (DEO) to transfer Mr. Dhoriya first, thus jumping the line. This act of manipulation not only left Mr. Dhoriya at a disadvantage but also betrayed the trust and friendship they had shared. It was a calculated move, one that would have upset many and left them questioning the integrity of others. Mr. Dhoriya, however, did not allow anger, bitterness, or resentment to cloud his judgment. He could have easily retaliated, resorted to conflict, or even sought revenge. Yet, his response was one of profound grace and patience.

Rather than resorting to a confrontation, Mr. Dhoriya chose to accept the injustice quietly. He saw it not as a personal affront but as a challenge to his own principles. He did not allow the deceit to compromise his values, nor did he allow it to dictate his emotional state. Instead, he remained composed, steadfast in his belief that the universe would deliver its own judgment in time. He knew that the path of integrity might be more difficult, but it was ultimately the one that would bring fulfilment and peace.

Over time, the consequences of the betrayal unfolded. Mr. Dhoriya's colleague, who had acted out of selfishness, soon began to experience the toll of his deceit. His health deteriorated, his relationships grew strained, and his life, which once seemed full of promise, began to unravel. In contrast, Mr. Dhoriya remained healthy, focused, and at peace. He continued to follow the path of integrity, unshaken by the betrayal that had occurred.

The comparison between the two men—one who had chosen the path of deceit and the other who had chosen guilelessness—serves as a powerful reminder that the strength of character lies not in one's ability to manipulate or deceive but in one's commitment to truth. While manipulation may offer temporary advantages, it is only truth and integrity that provide lasting strength and fulfilment. Mr. Dhoriya's response to betrayal is a testament to the power of guilelessness—a quiet, unspoken strength that allows one to weather the storms of life without losing their moral compass.

Personal Life: The Virtue of Fidelity and Patience in Marriage

If there is one area of Mr. Dhoriya's life where his commitment to guilelessness is most evident, it is in his personal relationships—specifically, in his marriage. His marriage to his wife is a poignant example of how guilelessness and integrity can transform relationships. His wife, though uneducated and at times difficult, has found in Mr. Dhoriya a partner who accepts her fully, without seeking to change her. Their relationship is built on mutual respect, trust, and deep patience, qualities that are at the heart of any lasting partnership.

Mr. Dhoriya's wife, though she may not share the same educational background, has never been made to feel inferior or excluded. In their marriage, Mr. Dhoriya has always been committed to being present, listening to her, and treating her as an equal partner in their shared life. This is a stark contrast to the often hierarchical nature of many relationships, where power dynamics or educational status can lead to feelings of alienation or disrespect.

Despite the challenges in their marriage—particularly due to his wife's strong-willed nature and lack of formal education—Mr. Dhoriya has never wavered in his commitment. He does not view his wife's imperfections as obstacles but rather as aspects of her that he deeply respects. His approach to marriage is based on fidelity, compassion, and the belief that true love requires acceptance, not transformation.

In an era where infidelity is unfortunately common, Mr. Dhoriya has remained steadfast in his dedication to his wife. Even in the face of temptations or the pressures that often come with his profession, he has remained unwavering in his commitment to her. His fidelity is not simply a matter of societal expectations or moral obligation but stems from a deeply personal conviction that true love is built on trust, loyalty, and respect.

Mr. Dhoriya's devotion to his wife, both emotionally and physically, serves as a remarkable example in a world where relationships often buckle under external pressures. His ability to remain emotionally connected and invested in his marriage, despite the difficulties they have faced, is a rare and admirable trait. He has never sought validation or affection from external sources but has focused his emotional energy on nurturing and strengthening the bond with his wife. His emotional fidelity further reflects his commitment to guilelessness—a devotion to truth, respect, and loyalty in all aspects of life.

The Enduring Power of Truth: A Life Well Lived

Mr. Dhoriya's life is an embodiment of the enduring power of truth. In a world where success is often measured by wealth, influence, and power, his life serves as a powerful reminder that the true measure of a person lies not in what they accumulate but in the integrity with which they live. His commitment to guilelessness is not just a personal virtue but also a reflection of a broader philosophical belief—that truth, honesty, and integrity are the bedrock of a meaningful and fulfilled life.

As Mr. Dhoriya looks back on his life, it is clear that the strength of his character has sustained him through both the good and bad times. His refusal to engage in deception or manipulation has allowed him to navigate the complexities of life with grace, dignity, and purpose. Amid a society that frequently praises those who cheat or take shortcuts, Mr. Dhoriya's life serves as a powerful reminder that true greatness is not defined by what we accomplish, but by the person we decide to become.

Through his unwavering commitment to guilelessness, Mr. Dhoriya has built a life that will endure long after his time. His story is not one of grand gestures or fleeting fame, but of quiet, consistent choices that reflect the strength of his character. His legacy is one of authenticity, integrity, and the enduring power of truth.

In the end, Mr. Dhoriya's life reminds us all that the greatest accomplishment is not achieving worldly success but remaining true to ourselves, staying grounded in our values, and living with guilelessness in a world that often demands more. Through his choices, Mr. Dhoriya has left an indelible mark—a mark not defined by external achievements but by the strength of his character and the truth that he carried within him.

XIII
Considerateness

*"It is commonly said that revenge is sweet, but to a calm
and considerate mind, patience and forgiveness are sweeter."*
- Isaac Barrow

Throughout his life, Mr. Dhoriya has embodied a
profound sense of considerateness that has never wavered,
no matter the circumstances. In an environment where
self-interest often obscures the genuine desire to act with
kindness and empathy towards others, Mr. Dhoriya shines
as a rare beacon of virtue. His heart beats not only for his
own survival but for the well-being of those around him,
even at the cost of his own comfort. The quality of being
kind is not merely an act for him, but a mode of existence,
so deeply woven into the fabric of his character that it flows
effortlessly through every interaction, whether mundane
or extraordinary. It is this deep-seated consideration for
others that has made Mr. Dhoriya a true pillar of his
community and an enduring source of inspiration for those
privileged to know him.

In a society increasingly defined by individualism and competition, where people often place their own success and happiness above the needs of others, Mr. Dhoriya's life presents a striking contrast. His actions are guided by a sense of duty and empathy that extends far beyond mere social niceties or superficial acts of charity. For Mr. Dhoriya, considerateness is not a transient quality but a way of life—a fundamental aspect of his character that shapes the way he interacts with the world. It is the thread that ties together his relationships, his work, and his legacy.

There are innumerable instances of Mr. Dhoriya's remarkable kindness, yet some stand out as profound illustrations of his essence. One such example occurred when his dear friend, whom we shall call R.K. Maheshwari, experienced the unbearable loss of his wife at a tragically young age. The woman, barely 40 years old, succumbed to a fever, leaving behind not only a grief-stricken husband but also two teenage children, adrift in their sorrow. The loss was shattering, and the grief that enveloped his friend was palpable. Yet, while the mourning was a deeply personal affair, marked by the silence and isolation that grief often brings, Mr. Dhoriya did not let his friend face the darkness alone.

The Act of Constant Presence in Grief

In the days following the death, when many would have, in the usual course of social interactions, visited only once or twice, offering their condolences and retreating back into the rhythm of their own lives, Mr. Dhoriya's sense of duty to his friend was unwavering. He visited R.K. Maheshwari every single day for twelve consecutive days, as tradition and cultural custom dictated, never once faltering in his dedication. There was no grand gesture, no public display of his actions, and yet, it was a rare and noble feat—one that required the kind of commitment that most would find difficult to offer.

In those quiet moments of conversation, Mr. Dhoriya did not simply offer words of consolation. His actions spoke louder than words; he provided a steady presence, soothing the raw edges of his friend's grief. With his characteristic patience, Mr. Dhoriya would listen to Maheshwari's reflections, his fears, and his anger at the cruel hand that fate had dealt him. There were no promises of a brighter future, no hollow words of "everything will be fine." Instead, Mr. Dhoriya offered something far more meaningful—an empathetic ear, and a heart that understood the depth of pain and sorrow.

What was most remarkable was not only the duration of Mr. Dhoriya's support but the nature of it. While many people in his position might have offered their condolences and moved on with their lives, Mr. Dhoriya's commitment to remain by his friend's side was unwavering. He understood that grief is not a one-time event but a process—one that requires continuous support and understanding. His actions were a testament to his belief that true friendship means being there for someone when they need you the most, even when it is inconvenient, even when it demands personal sacrifice.

Selflessness in Action: When Time Becomes a Gift

It may seem a small thing to visit a mourning friend for twelve days, but in this world that has become ever more self-centred, where time is a commodity and lives are lived in constant motion, such an act reveals a quality so rare, it deserves deep reflection. To prioritize another's sorrow over one's own convenience, to give of oneself without expectation of anything in return, is a testament to the depth of Mr. Dhoriya's character. His time, often in short supply due to his own commitments, was offered selflessly, as a gesture of empathy that can never be quantified.

Considerateness, in this case, was not about providing grand solutions to the problem of grief, which is ultimately a personal journey. Instead, it was about offering the invaluable gift of time, presence, and empathy. In an era where people often hurry to fix problems or ease discomfort, Mr. Dhoriya's willingness to simply be present for his friend served as a reminder of the true power of human connection. It is often the smallest acts, like a steady presence during times of suffering that leave the most lasting impact.

The Land Incident: A Test of Ethics and Integrity

Another telling example of Mr. Dhoriya's profound considerateness lies in the way he approached his relationship with the land. The place he calls home is situated next to a parcel of land that, though legally questionable, has been occupied by its owners for years. This land, which would have cost Mr. Dhoriya a mere fraction of what his own plot was worth, might have been an easy acquisition for someone in his position. After all, it was a valuable piece of real estate, and those with the financial means often find ways to make such transactions work in their favour. But Mr. Dhoriya, unlike many, chose not to take advantage of this opportunity.

The idea of acquiring land in such a manner did not sit well with his conscience. His decision was not born out of a simple desire for personal morality; rather, it stemmed from a deeply rooted respect for the sanctity of land itself. To him, land was not a mere commodity to be bought and sold—it was a symbol of life, heritage, and law. The idea that one might dishonour the sanctity of the land by pursuing an illegitimate claim to it was something Mr. Dhoriya could not accept.

A Commitment to Honoring the Natural Order

Mr. Dhoriya's decision to respect the boundaries of what was right, even at the expense of his own potential gain, revealed a deep commitment to considerateness—not just in terms of other people but also in regard to the very laws and moral guidelines that govern society. His unwavering respect for the law, and his belief in the ethical treatment of property, meant that he could not act in a manner that would disturb the natural order, even if the financial gain might have been substantial.

In this case, Mr. Dhoriya was not acting out of a desire for recognition or praise. His actions were not driven by a need to appear virtuous but by an internal compass that guided him to do what was right, regardless of the personal cost. For him, considerateness extended beyond human interactions; it encompassed the broader web of relationships—whether with land, laws, or society at large—that contribute to the common good.

The Path of Service: True Leadership

Yet, perhaps the most telling expression of Mr. Dhoriya's considerateness lies in his unwavering commitment to social responsibility. Mr. Dhoriya has never been one to seek titles, recognition, or accolades in his community. There are those who vie for positions of power, those who wish to adorn themselves with the honours of their social circles, but Mr. Dhoriya has never been drawn to such ambitions. Instead, his focus has always been on the work itself. It is the task that calls him, not the recognition. His sense of responsibility, his desire to make a meaningful contribution to society, has always been rooted in the desire to serve others without expecting anything in return.

For Mr. Dhoriya, the true reward of service lies not in public acknowledgment but in the quiet satisfaction of knowing that he has made a difference in the lives of others. He believes that the highest form of leadership is not to command but to serve, not to dominate but to lift others up. This philosophy has guided him throughout his life and has led him to consistently choose paths that prioritize the welfare of others over his own personal gain.

The Essence of True Leadership

His work has never been driven by personal gain. He has always taken on the most difficult and thankless tasks, laboring not for rewards or accolades but for the simple satisfaction of doing what is right. This is a man who has understood, perhaps better than most that true leadership is not about prestige or power but about service, humility, and a commitment to the common good.

What I have observed in him over the years is an unwavering adherence to the righteous path, not for the purpose of grandstanding or self-glorification, but because it is the only path he knows. His actions speak louder than any words he could ever utter. He does not need to trumpet his virtue from the rooftops—his life itself is a testament to the quiet strength of character that he carries with him. His approach to life is not about achieving external recognition but about staying true to his core values, regardless of external pressures or temptations.

A Beacon of Light in an Increasingly Self-Centered World

In a world that often seems preoccupied with the pursuit of material wealth and status, Mr. Dhoriya stands as a rare and noble exception. His considerateness is not a mere quality to be admired—it is a lesson to be learned. It is a reminder that, no matter how modern or fast-paced the world becomes, we must never lose sight of the fundamental values that make us human: kindness, empathy, respect for others, and a deep commitment to serving the greater good.

Through his life, Mr. Dhoriya has shown us that true greatness is not measured by what we accumulate but by what we give. It is the quiet, often unacknowledged acts of kindness that leave the deepest impression and create the most lasting impact. His life is a testament to the idea that the most powerful force we have in this life is the power to care for one another. By living with such considerateness, Mr. Dhoriya has not only improved the lives of those around him but has also set an example for all of us to follow—a model of how we can contribute to the well-being of our communities and the world at large.

The Legacy of Considerateness

As we look at the example Mr. Dhoriya has set, we are reminded of the profound impact that a life lived with consideration can have—not only on the individuals we touch but on the world at large. His life, though humble, is a beacon of hope in an increasingly self-centred world. In a society that often values efficiency, power, and material success above all else, Mr. Dhoriya's life shows us that true fulfilment comes not from what we gain, but from how we serve others. Through his actions, he has taught us that kindness, empathy, and a genuine commitment to the well-being of others are the cornerstones of a meaningful and impactful life.

XIV

Receptiveness

"A mind is like a parachute. It doesn't work if it's not open." -
Frank Zappa

The most precious quality that one can possess—one that transcends the material and the superficial and penetrates the very core of human connection—is the ability to listen. To truly listen, to be receptive to the voices that cry out in pain, in joy, in confusion, and in hope, is to offer the most profound and selfless form of empathy. Mr. Dhoriya, throughout the tapestry of his life, has embodied this rare and invaluable trait with remarkable consistency. Receptiveness is more than a quality for him; it is a way of being—a philosophy that guides him in every interaction, large or small, and infuses his relationships with a depth of understanding that is both rare and profound.

In a world that often emphasizes individualism, personal achievement, and the pursuit of one's own goals, Mr. Dhoriya's capacity for receptiveness is a breath of fresh air. It is a quality that is too often overshadowed by the noise of self-interest, yet he has remained steadfast in his ability to listen—not just with his ears, but with his heart. For him, to listen is to offer not just advice, but presence—a calm, steady, and unwavering source of support that others can lean on in their darkest hours. This ability to listen, to absorb the pain and joy of others, and to respond with genuine empathy is what has made him a pillar of support to all who have sought his counsel.

The Story of Shivji Siju

One of the most poignant examples of Mr. Dhoriya's receptiveness comes from his relationship with his relative, a man whom I shall refer to as Shivji Siju. Shivji's life had been a series of misfortunes, each one compounding the next. Burdened by the weight of despair and struggling with an addiction to alcohol, Shivji found himself at the mercy of his own mind, caught in a spiral of negative thoughts and hopelessness. The solace he sought in drinking only led him further into darkness, creating a distance between him and those who loved him.

More than once, Shivji's suffering reached a point where he considered the most final of decisions: ending his life. It was in these moments of crisis that Mr. Dhoriya stepped in, unwavering in his resolve to offer a listening ear, a steady voice, and, most importantly, a sense of hope that transcended the boundaries of despair. Whenever the call came—sometimes in the late hours of the night, when the silence of the world outside was only rivalled by the turmoil within Shivji's heart—Mr. Dhoriya would answer. His voice was always calm, reassuring, full of understanding, but never dismissive of the gravity of Shivji's situation.

Mr. Dhoriya's ability to offer empathy and presence in the face of such deep sorrow remains a powerful testament to the transformative power of receptiveness.

The Story of Nimesh and His Family

Another example that highlights Mr. Dhoriya's receptiveness can be found in the story of Nimesh, a young man who was deeply infatuated with a girl from his community. Nimesh's affection for the girl, whom I will refer to as the bride, had grown into something more serious. Both families, the bride's and Nimesh's, were aware of the budding romance, and at first, both sides seemed content with the idea of a union. However, complications arose when the bride's family, particularly her parents, became unsure of the match. There were unresolved tensions within the bride's family—long-standing familial disturbances that cast doubt on the possibility of a peaceful marriage. The young woman, under the weight of these pressures, eventually decided to decline the proposal, and the wedding plans were abruptly called off.

In this delicate and volatile situation, many might have rushed to impose their opinions, push for reconciliation, or perhaps, in frustration, turned their backs. However, Mr. Dhoriya, with his quiet wisdom, did none of these things. Instead, he remained calm, observant, and most importantly, receptive to the unfolding circumstances. He recognized that this was a matter that required careful handling—one that demanded patience, understanding, and an ability to see beyond the surface.

Rather than revealing the bride's decision to Nimesh immediately, Mr. Dhoriya chose to wait. He understood that in matters of the heart, emotions could be fragile and that a hasty revelation could cause unnecessary hurt or turmoil. Instead, he gave both families the time they needed to reflect, to resolve their differences, and to come to a decision in their own time. During this period, he remained a quiet but steadfast support, offering guidance and understanding when necessary, but never forcing his hand or imposing his own desires onto the situation.

Over time, as tensions in the bride's family eased and the issues that had once stood in the way of the union were addressed, the situation gradually began to clear. Eventually, both sides of the family came together in agreement, and the marriage took place—a union that, although delayed, was ultimately one of mutual happiness and understanding. Mr. Dhoriya's ability to listen, to allow the situation to unfold without rushing it, and to guide others through their own emotional maelstrom was a testament to his profound receptiveness. He understood that sometimes, the most important thing one can offer is not an answer, but the space to find one.

The Rare Quality of Receptiveness

In a society that often glorifies quick fixes, decisive actions, and the loud voices of those who aim to impose their will on others, Mr. Dhoriya's receptiveness stands out as a rare and remarkable virtue. It is a quality that requires patience and emotional intelligence, a willingness to step back and allow others to speak their truths, no matter how difficult or uncomfortable. Mr. Dhoriya's receptiveness is not just about hearing the words spoken by others—it is about understanding the silences between the words, the unspoken pain, the quiet fears, and the hopes that lie hidden beneath the surface.

In the many years I have observed him, I have come to realize that Mr. Dhoriya's capacity to listen, to truly hear, is a gift he has shared not only with those in his immediate circle but with all who have crossed his path. Whether it was the troubled relative, the conflicted young couple, or anyone else in need, he has always been there to offer his presence, his understanding, and his unwavering support. In doing so, he has touched lives in ways that words alone cannot fully express.

To listen is to offer a silent form of compassion, one that transcends the boundaries of speech and taps into the deepest parts of our shared humanity. Mr. Dhoriya's life is a testament to the power of receptiveness—to the idea that sometimes, the greatest gift we can give is our attention, our empathy, and our willingness to be present in the lives of those who need us the most. In his quiet, steadfast way, he has shown us all that to be receptive is to be human, and in doing so, he has illuminated the path to a more compassionate, understanding world.

A Quiet Influence

Mr. Dhoriya's receptiveness has not only shaped his personal relationships but has also made him an influential figure in his community. His quiet, humble demeanour stands in stark contrast to the louder, more attention-grabbing personalities often seen in positions of authority.

Yet, it is precisely this gentle, attentive nature that has made him such a powerful presence in the lives of those who have sought his guidance.

His ability to listen to people, to understand their struggles, and to offer advice when needed, has earned him the deep respect and affection of everyone around him. He has been a steady anchor for many in the community, offering support when people have needed it the most. Whether it was a young couple seeking guidance in their relationship or an elderly person struggling with feelings of loneliness, Mr. Dhoriya's receptiveness has allowed him to serve as a counsellor and confidant to all who have sought his wisdom.

Unlike many who might offer quick solutions or try to fix problems with hasty decisions, Mr. Dhoriya's approach has always been more patient and measured. He listens, absorbs, and then responds—not with judgments or preconceived notions, but with the kind of insight that comes from truly understanding the situation at hand. It is this rare ability to offer a space for people to express themselves fully, without fear of criticism or dismissal, that has made Mr. Dhoriya such a cherished presence in the lives of so many.

The Power of Presence

What sets Mr. Dhoriya apart is not just his ability to listen, but his power of presence. To be truly present with someone, to give them your undivided attention and emotional energy, is a gift that cannot be overstated. In a world where distractions are everywhere and people often communicate through technology rather than face-to-face interaction, Mr. Dhoriya has preserved the art of being fully present. When someone speaks to him, they have his complete focus—there is no rush, no impatience, just a quiet willingness to hear them out.

This power of presence has allowed him to build deep, trusting relationships with people from all walks of life. It has made him someone who is relied upon, respected, and loved, not just for his wisdom but for his unwavering commitment to being there for others. Through his receptiveness, he has taught us all the profound impact of truly listening, of giving others the space to be heard, and of offering compassion without expectation.

In conclusion, Mr. Dhoriya's receptiveness is not just a characteristic—it is a way of being that has touched the lives of many. His ability to listen, to offer comfort without judgment, and to create a space where others can find their own answers, is a gift that has made him a beacon of support, understanding, and compassion. In a world that often values speed and efficiency over empathy and presence, Mr. Dhoriya reminds us all of the transformative power of truly listening and being present with one another. Through his life and his example, he has illuminated the path to a more compassionate, thoughtful world.

XV
Sobriety

"If you could learn how to be drunk all the time and fully alert, wouldn't you be interested?"
—**Sadguru (Jaggi Vasudev)**

In the ever-changing currents of human existence, where desires surge and ebb like the ceaseless tides of an unpredictable ocean, there lies a virtue that holds steadfast and unyielding against the overwhelming onslaught of indulgence: sobriety. It is not merely a condition of abstaining from external intoxicants, but rather a profound and transformative state of being that transcends the material realm. Sobriety, in its truest form, is an embodiment of clarity and balance—both of the mind and of the body. In an age where the allure of momentary pleasures tempts the senses and distracts the soul, the disciplined and enlightened soul who chooses sobriety walks with an inner radiance, untouched by the passing storms of worldly distractions. Mr. Dhoriya, a man whose life is an eloquent expression of simplicity and intellectual clarity, has made sobriety his guiding light—an unwavering commitment to the path of spiritual growth and mental clarity.

The notion of sobriety, far from being a mere personal choice or a passing trend, is deeply spiritual, embedded in the very teachings of the great wisdom traditions of humanity. Across cultures, philosophies, and religions, there runs a common thread that extols the value of self-restraint, mindfulness, and moderation in the face of life's temptations. The universal call to transcend excess, to tame the fleeting desires of the body, and to cultivate a serene and undisturbed mind is not confined to any one tradition; rather, it resonates through the annals of human civilization as a timeless and ageless truth. In this chapter, we will explore how the great teachings of Hinduism, Islam, and Christianity—each with its unique lens on spirituality—advocate for the transformative power of sobriety. Through these lenses, we will also come to understand how Mr. Dhoriya's life is a modern embodiment of these age-old principles, showing us that sobriety is not a mere absence of indulgence but a presence of higher wisdom, peace, and fulfilment.

The Teachings of Hinduism

In Hinduism, the concept of addiction, though not always articulated in contemporary terms, finds its roots in the attachment to desires—Kama—which ultimately leads to spiritual bondage. The Bhagavad Gita, the philosophical and spiritual masterpiece that has guided millions through the labyrinth of life's complexities, speaks eloquently about the perils of unchecked desires. The Gita, a guide to the deeper mysteries of human existence, presents the idea that suffering arises when an individual becomes ensnared by the constant pull of sensory indulgence. In its divine wisdom, it teaches that when the mind becomes dominated by sensory craving, one is pulled away from the true essence of the self—atman—and diverted from the path of self-realization.

Lord Krishna, in his dialogue with Arjuna, advises relinquishment of attachment to the fruits of one's actions, encouraging a life centred on duty, righteousness, and the pursuit of higher consciousness. Through this pursuit, one must transcend the temporary pleasures that arise from sensory indulgences, cultivating instead the discipline of self-restraint. The Gita speaks of a life that is free from the tyranny of desire—samyak darshan—a life of balance and moderation in which true liberation (moksha) can be attained.

In the life of Mr. Dhoriya, we see the clear reflection of these ancient teachings. His life is a testament to the practice of moderation—seeking knowledge, spiritual growth, and wisdom over fleeting pleasures. Mr. Dhoriya, much like Arjuna in the Gita, recognizes that while the pleasures of the material world may offer temporary gratification, they ultimately lead to a deeper sense of emptiness. Spiritual fulfilment, by contrast, offers lasting peace and wisdom—an understanding that is not only internalized but also lived by. This adherence to the principles of moderation and self-discipline is not merely intellectual for Mr. Dhoriya; it is a living, breathing philosophy that informs every aspect of his life. In choosing to abstain from the allure of material indulgence, he demonstrates a deeper commitment to the pursuit of moksha—the liberation of the soul from the cycle of desire and suffering.

The Teachings of Islam

Islam, too, holds a firm stance against addiction, viewing it as an insidious form of attachment that leads one away from the straight path of righteousness. In the Qur'an, the concept of excess—whether in food, drink, or other worldly indulgences—is explicitly condemned. Surah Al-A'raf (7:31) offers profound guidance, saying, "O children of Adam! Take your adornment at every masjid and eat and drink, but be not excessive. Indeed, He likes not those who commit excess." This verse encapsulates a broader Islamic philosophy: that moderation is the key to a righteous life. Excess, in any form, pulls the individual away from the worship of Allah, from submission to His will, and from the balanced, harmonious life that is the ultimate goal of Islam.

The Qur'an, therefore, teaches not only about the harms of overindulgence but also about the benefits of self-restraint. The strength to control one's desires, to act with mindfulness and discipline, is seen as a reflection of submission to the will of Allah. True freedom, according to Islamic teachings, does not lie in the pursuit of sensory pleasure but in the ability to transcend these pleasures in favour of spiritual fulfilment and devotion.

Mr. Dhoriya's life exemplifies this Islamic principle. He has chosen a life of temperance, where discipline is paramount. He has rejected the intoxicating allure of worldly pleasures—whether it be the overindulgence of food, drink, or other forms of excess. Instead, his focus remains steadfast on his duty and spiritual development. His actions reflect the Islamic concept of self-control, where the individual does not succumb to the whims of the body but rather aligns every action with a higher purpose: the pursuit of spiritual growth, peace, and unity with the divine.

The Teachings of Christianity

Christianity, too, speaks to the dangers of addiction, framing it as a form of enslavement to both the desires of the flesh and the temptations of sin. In the New Testament, the Apostle Paul directly addresses this issue, urging believers to free themselves from the chains of addiction and sin: "Let not sin therefore reign in your mortal body, to make you obey its passions. Do not present your members to sin as instruments for unrighteousness, but present yourselves to God as those who have been brought from death to life" (Romans 6:12-13). In this, Christianity presents addiction not only as a form of physical enslavement but also as a spiritual bondage—a diversion from the higher calling of righteousness and divine peace.

In Christian thought, true freedom comes not from self-reliance or willpower alone but through the grace of God. It is through divine intervention—the presence of the Holy

Spirit—that an individual finds the strength to resist temptation and rise above the addictive tendencies that seek to bind the soul. The process of overcoming addiction is viewed as a journey of spiritual transformation, where believers are guided by the strength and wisdom that comes from a connection with God.

Although Mr. Dhoriya is not necessarily a practicing Christian, he intuitively embraces this principle of liberation. His commitment to abstaining from worldly indulgences and his focus on spiritual fulfilment mirror the Christian idea of freedom from sin and addiction. Like a true disciple, Mr. Dhoriya has made a conscious choice to resist the pull of earthly temptations. He has learned that true peace and contentment do not arise from the indulgence of the senses but from cultivating a deep and abiding connection with one's higher self and purpose.

Mr. Dhoriya's Personal Commitment to Sobriety

For Mr. Dhoriya, sobriety is not a theoretical concept but a lived experience—one that is woven into the very fabric of his daily life. His commitment to abstaining from indulgences is not a mere act of self-denial but an affirmation of his spiritual and intellectual growth. In his youth, Mr. Dhoriya experimented with smoking, but he quickly realized that it, like other indulgences, offered no true satisfaction. The fleeting euphoria it provided was overshadowed by the deeper truth that it served only to perpetuate false desires. Smoking, like other addictions, is but a momentary escape—a distraction from the deeper yearning of the soul for peace and wisdom. Recognizing this, Mr. Dhoriya chose to leave it behind, and in doing so, he demonstrated a deep understanding of the Buddhist principle of detachment.

Mr. Dhoriya is a living example of the Buddha's teaching that one must practice what they preach. He does not advocate for sobriety because it is fashionable or doctrinally correct; he does so because it is a truth he has experienced firsthand. His life is an embodiment of the principle that true freedom is not found in the pursuit of external pleasures, but in the cultivation of inner peace and spiritual growth.

The Nature of True Joy

In Mr. Dhoriya's life, we see that true joy is not dependent on the fleeting pleasures of the material world. His joy is found in the serenity that emanates from within, a deep and abiding contentment that comes from knowing oneself and living in alignment with one's higher purpose. This joy, unlike the temporary pleasures of indulgence, is constant and enduring—untouched by external circumstances. In Mr. Dhoriya's presence, one is enveloped in an aura of tranquillity, as though he carries within him a wellspring of joy that no external force can diminish. This is the true intoxication—the intoxication of the spirit that arises from an intimate connection with the deeper truths of existence.

In an environment often captivated by the allure of indulgence and fleeting pleasures, Mr. Dhoriya shines as a beacon of sobriety and spiritual wisdom. His life is a testament to the idea that true fulfilment does not lie in external pleasures, but in the cultivation of inner peace and spiritual clarity. Guided by the timeless principles of moderation and mindfulness found in Hinduism, Islam, and Christianity, Mr. Dhoriya offers a powerful example of how to navigate the complexities of modern life without being consumed by its distractions. His unwavering commitment to sobriety reveals a deeper truth: that sobriety is not the absence of excess, but the presence of something far greater—a peace that transcends the ephemeral and leads to lasting fulfilment.

XVI

Respect

"A Person's a person, no matter how small."- Dr. Seuss.

Respect is a virtue that transcends time, culture, and social boundaries. It is universally acknowledged as a cornerstone of good character, a quality that defines a person's integrity and moral compass. The act of respecting others is not merely a gesture or superficial action—it is a deliberate, active expression of empathy, understanding, and appreciation for the inherent dignity of every individual. Respect is a fundamental aspect of human interactions and relationships. A truly respectful person is one whose actions, words, and behaviour consistently reflect an understanding of the value and worth of others, regardless of their background, status, or personal circumstances.

Being respectful is more than just good manners or politeness. It requires intentionality and self-awareness. It involves recognizing that every person has a story, a history, and a set of unique experiences that shape who they are.

A respectful person listens attentively, seeks to understand, and, above all, treats others with fairness and kindness. This type of respect is earned over time, through consistent actions that demonstrate care and consideration for others. It is a value that transcends social and cultural norms, a universal language that brings people together and fosters unity.

Mr. Mr. Dhoriya, the central figure in this book, is a living embodiment of this ideal of respect. Throughout his long and distinguished career as a teacher, he consistently demonstrated an unwavering commitment to treating others with dignity and understanding. His life and work are a testament to the power of respect and its transformative impact on individuals and communities. For Mr. Dhoriya, respect was not a mere formality or societal expectation; it was a deeply ingrained principle that guided his every interaction.

In this chapter, we will explore how Mr. Dhoriya personified the essence of respect in both his professional and personal life. Through a series of real-life examples and anecdotes, we will see how his approach to respect transcended the conventional understanding of this virtue. Mr. Dhoriya's legacy is a testament to the enduring power of respect to heal, unite, and uplift individuals from all walks of life.

The Community of Legacy and Respect

India's diverse social fabric is home to numerous communities with rich cultural traditions and legacies. These communities often have unique values that shape the ways in which individuals within them interact with others. One such community, belonging to a particular sect of Hinduism, has long been known for its reverence for others. This tradition of respect is passed down through generations, instilling a deep sense of empathy, humility, and consideration for others. Within the context of DV High School, where Mr. Dhoriya taught for many years, this community was a significant presence.

The school, with its diverse student body, often witnessed tensions between different groups. These tensions, often arising from socio-economic, cultural, or religious differences, sometimes led to conflicts and divisions among the students. However, there was one constant in the midst of these challenges: whenever discord arose, the members of this particular community would turn to Mr. Dhoriya for guidance and resolution. His reputation for fairness, approachability, and integrity made him the natural choice for mediating such conflicts.

Despite being a relatively quiet and reserved community, the students within this group held Mr. Dhoriya in high regard. Their respect for him was not born out of fear or obligation, but from a deep recognition of the values he embodied—values that resonated with their own. When conflicts erupted within the student body, Mr. Dhoriya remained neutral, always ensuring that he listened to all parties involved before offering his counsel. His calm demeanour and unwavering principles created an atmosphere of trust and understanding, which allowed for meaningful dialogue and conflict resolution.

The students from this community found in Mr. Dhoriya a figure who mirrored the values they held dear—values of humility, justice, and respect. His ability to mediate and bring about peace in tense situations demonstrated the profound impact that respect can have on even the most volatile of circumstances. Through his example, these students learned the importance of approaching others with kindness and fairness, regardless of their differences.

The Case of Govind: Respect amidst Chaos

One of the most compelling examples of Mr. Dhoriya's ability to command respect and defuse tense situations occurred with a student named Govind. Govind was a notorious figure at DV High School during the early 2000s. At 22 years old, he was several years older than his peers, and his reputation was that of a troublemaker, involved in numerous violent altercations both inside and outside the school. He had been linked to more than ten criminal cases, most of them related to gang violence and confrontations with rival students. Govind's presence was often a source of fear and anxiety among both students and teachers alike.

When a violent gang confrontation erupted at the school, Govind was at the centre of the chaos. Teachers, who were understandably apprehensive about getting involved in such a volatile situation, would often avoid confrontation or resort to punitive measures. But Mr. Dhoriya's response was different. He did not react with anger or authority, nor did he seek to impose his will on Govind through intimidation. Instead, he approached the situation with a quiet yet firm sense of respect. When he spoke to Govind, his tone was calm and non-judgmental, acknowledging the young man's frustrations without condoning his violent behaviour.

To everyone's surprise, Govind, known for his rebellious and combative nature, instantly calmed down. His previously tense posture relaxed, and he lowered his gaze in a gesture of submission. He agreed to a truce, not through coercion, but through a simple exchange of mutual respect. Govind, despite his history of violence, recognized in Mr. Dhoriya a figure who treated him as an individual, not as a criminal or a troublemaker. In this moment, Mr. Dhoriya demonstrated the true power of respect: the ability to connect with others on a human level, to see beyond their flaws and imperfections, and to inspire positive change through empathy and understanding.

This remarkable encounter is just one example of how Mr. Dhoriya's approach to respect allowed him to defuse potentially explosive situations. He understood that respect was not about exerting power over others, but about acknowledging their humanity and treating them with dignity, no matter their past actions. His ability to reach Govind, a student who had alienated many others, shows the transformative effect that respect can have on even the most difficult individuals.

Handling the Media: Respect in the Face of Adversity

As a teacher at a prominent institution, Mr. Dhoriya was often called upon to handle difficult situations that involved the media. One such instance occurred when the school's CCTV cameras were stolen during a robbery. The incident was quickly picked up by the media, and reporters began to swarm the school in search of information. Most people would have responded to such an intrusion with defensiveness or frustration, particularly given the potentially damaging nature of the story. However, Mr. Dhoriya took a different approach.

Rather than react with hostility or attempt to avoid the media, he chose to engage with them respectfully. He understood that journalists had a job to do, and while their reports might not always be favorable, their role in society was important. When confronted by reporters, Mr. Dhoriya remained calm and composed, offering measured responses that acknowledged the facts without resorting to sensationalism or blame. He was transparent about the situation, recognizing that the media had a responsibility to inform the public, and he treated them with the same respect he would extend to any professional.

In doing so, Mr. Dhoriya not only preserved his own dignity but also maintained the integrity of the school. He demonstrated that respect is not limited to interpersonal relationships but extends to all interactions, even those that might be challenging or uncomfortable. By treating the media with respect, he ensured that the school's reputation remained intact, despite the negative attention it was receiving.

Respect and Popularity: An Inclusive Influence

One of the most striking aspects of Mr. Dhoriya's character was the breadth of respect he commanded. Unlike many individuals who are only respected by certain groups or circles, Mr. Dhoriya earned the admiration of people from all walks of life. His respect for others was not contingent on social status, personality, or background. Whether it was a teacher, a student, a parent, or a member of the community, everyone who interacted with Mr. Dhoriya felt valued and appreciated.

This widespread respect was not the result of superficial charm or flattery, but rather the outcome of Mr. Dhoriya's consistent and genuine efforts to treat others with kindness, fairness, and dignity. Even those who were naturally introverted or socially withdrawn felt comfortable around him. He created a space where individuals could express themselves freely, without fear of judgment or rejection. In this way, he fostered a sense of inclusivity at DV High School, where every individual was respected and made to feel like they belonged.

His popularity was not based on the desire for personal gain or recognition, but on the genuine respect he had for others. His example showed that true influence comes not from asserting power or authority, but from consistently demonstrating care and respect for those around you.

The Enduring Power of Respect

As we reflect on the life and legacy of Mr. Dhoriya, we are reminded of the enduring power of respect. It is a quality that can heal divisions, foster understanding, and inspire growth. Through his actions, Mr. Dhoriya demonstrated that respect is not simply a virtue to aspire to—it is a practice that must be cultivated and lived daily. His life stands as a powerful reminder that true respect is earned through consistent, compassionate action and that its impact can be far-reaching, touching the lives of all those with whom we interact.

In a setup often divided by differences, it is respect that has the power to bring us together. Mr. Dhoriya's story continues to inspire all who hear it, reminding us that the simple act of respecting others can transform lives, build bridges, and foster a more compassionate and harmonious world.

XVII

Benevolence

"He who nurtures benevolence for all creatures within his heart overcomes all difficulties and will be the recipient of all types of riches at every step." -Chanakya

Benevolence is not merely an act; it is a way of being. It is the radiant light that brightens the darkest corners of the world, an emanation of love and kindness that nourishes not only the soul of the giver but also the hearts of those fortunate enough to receive it. In its most elevated form, benevolence transcends boundaries—whether of caste, class, or creed—moving effortlessly from one soul to another, seeking no reward but itself. It is a force that works silently, continuously, leaving behind a legacy of goodwill that endures long after the actions have ceased. This is the essence of Mr. Mr. Dhoriya's character—a man whose life has been defined by the quiet strength of benevolence. In every moment, through every action, he has demonstrated that true generosity is not measured by grand gestures but by the consistency and selflessness with which we extend ourselves to others.

The Quiet Art of Giving

Mr. Dhoriya's life has never been driven by the pursuit of wealth or material possessions. From my earliest memories, I can attest to the fact that he has always placed value on people rather than things. While many in his position might indulge in the luxuries of life, Mr. Dhoriya has steadfastly resisted the urge to accumulate wealth for wealth's sake. His approach to life is simple yet profound: give where you can, without expectation of return. To him, material wealth is a tool—useful for meeting life's basic needs, but not the essence of a fulfilled existence.

Non-materialistic Philosophy

He has never been interested in buying expensive things for himself. While he certainly recognizes the utility of material possessions, he sees them as transient objects, of little lasting value. Yet, if he is gifted something—particularly by family—he accepts it with gratitude and humility, as if to remind us all that love, not objects, is what sustains us.

The Significance of Giving Without Expectation

One of the most striking aspects of his generosity is his willingness to give without attachment. He has always been quick to lend assistance to others, but he does so with the understanding that once money is lent, it should be forgotten. He never burdens himself with the expectation that it will be returned. In his view, to hold onto the desire for repayment is to risk unnecessary stress, for money is not a source of security—it is merely a tool to facilitate life's needs.

Acts of Generosity: Transforming Lives Through Small Gestures

Benevolence in Mr. Dhoriya's life is never confined to grand or ostentatious acts. Instead, his generosity manifests itself in small, seemingly inconsequential moments that, when accumulated, have a profound and lasting impact on those around him. One such example is his relationship with his former students.

a) The Case of Jeetu: A Memory that Endures

During a particularly trying period when his son was ill and hospitalized due to dengue fever, Mr. Dhoriya encountered a compounder named Jeetu, who was also once his student. Jeetu shared with us an unforgettable memory from his school days. He recalled how, as a young boy without even the basic necessity of a pair of sandals, he was given a new pair by Mr. Dhoriya without hesitation. Jeetu's recollection of this simple but significant act speaks volumes about the kind of person Mr. Dhoriya is: someone whose generosity is not measured by the magnitude of the gift but by the thoughtfulness and immediacy with which it is given.

b) The Scholarship Scheme: A Personal Commitment

Another vivid example of Mr. Dhoriya's generosity is his involvement in ensuring that underprivileged students, particularly those from the SC/ST communities, received the government scholarships meant to help them continue their education. These schemes, though significant, are often overlooked by students who are unaware of their existence or too burdened by life's challenges to claim them. Mr. Dhoriya would often go out of his way, visiting the homes of these students to remind them of the opportunity available to them. This act of kindness, though seemingly small, speaks volumes about his commitment to the betterment of others, particularly the underprivileged. In a world that is increasingly indifferent to the struggles of others, such acts of selfless service are rare and should be celebrated.

The Gift of Time: An Irreplaceable Offering

While money is important, the one thing that is truly irreplaceable is time. Time, once spent, can never be reclaimed, and to dedicate it to another person is one of the greatest acts of benevolence one can offer.

a) Spending Time with a Neighbour in Need

One of the most remarkable aspects of Mr. Dhoriya's benevolence is his willingness to dedicate his time to others, particularly those in his community. I vividly recall one instance when a neighbor, who had recently been paralyzed, was grappling with the emotional and physical challenges of his new condition. Despite his own busy schedule, Mr. Dhoriya would visit him regularly, spending hours each day to provide comfort, encouragement, and a listening ear. These visits, which often involved nothing more than simple conversation, made an enormous difference in the neighbor's life. It was not just the physical presence of Mr. Dhoriya that was important, but the emotional and psychological support he provided—helping to restore a sense of hope and belonging.

b) Offering Unquestioning Support

Mr. Dhoriya has never been one to count the cost of his time. Whether it was assisting students with academic difficulties, offering advice to colleagues, or providing emotional support to those in distress, he has always been there. For him, time is an invaluable gift, one that can never be fully repaid, but which serves to forge lasting bonds between people. His willingness to give his time freely to others, even when his own responsibilities are overwhelming, speaks volumes about his character.

A Legacy of Kindness: The Ripple Effect of Benevolence

Benevolence, by its very nature, has a far-reaching impact. A single act of kindness can create a ripple effect, inspiring others to act with compassion and generosity in turn. Mr. Dhoriya's life has been a testament to this principle. His acts of generosity, though often small in scale, have created a legacy that continues to inspire those who know him.

a) Building a Culture of Giving

His example has inspired not only his family but also his colleagues, friends, and students. His belief in the power of giving—whether it is through the offering of material aid, time, or emotional support—has shaped the way many of us understand the value of service to others. In a world

Mr. Dhoriya would listen for hours, allowing Shivji to pour out his pain and confusion. In those moments, Mr. Dhoriya did not offer immediate solutions or preach any sort of doctrine. He simply listened. He allowed Shivji to express his deepest fears, his sense of powerlessness, and the crushing weight of his addiction. And through it all, Mr. Dhoriya's presence was a constant reminder that Shivji was not alone—that even in the depths of his despair, someone was there to walk beside him.

Though Mr. Dhoriya's words were always wise, gentle, and encouraging, they were never overbearing. He understood that, sometimes, the most healing thing one can offer is the simple act of being there. He knew that words alone could not always mend the deep wounds that Shivji carried, but his unwavering presence allowed Shivji to feel heard, to feel understood. It was in these moments that Mr. Dhoriya demonstrated the essence of receptiveness—not just as a quality, but as a practice of opening oneself to the suffering of another, and offering the space for healing, however small or incremental it might be.

But, tragically, despite all of Mr. Dhoriya's efforts, Shivji could not overcome the darkness within himself. One fateful day, he took his own life, leaving behind a family in grief. Mr. Dhoriya's heart broke for him, but even in this devastating outcome, he never wavered in his belief that he had done everything he could. He had been there, listening and offering comfort in the most profound way possible. And in doing so, he gave Shivji the greatest gift that any human being can offer: the gift of being heard. It is the nature of life that not every story has a happy ending, but increasingly consumed by individualism and self-interest, Mr. Dhoriya's life offers a refreshing reminder that true fulfillment lies not in what we accumulate but in what we give away.

b) Fostering a Spirit of Community

Beyond individual acts, Mr. Dhoriya has worked to foster a spirit of community wherever he goes. Through his quiet acts of kindness, he has built networks of support that transcend familial bonds, creating a ripple effect that extends into the broader community. Whether it is through organizing community events, mentoring students, or offering counsel to those in need, his life has been a model of how one person's actions can shape the collective good.

A Beacon of Hope

Mr. Dhoriya's life is a profound reminder that the essence of benevolence is not in the magnitude of our gestures, but in the consistency and selflessness with which we offer ourselves to others. His generosity, both material and emotional, has created ripples that continue to shape the lives of those who encounter him. In a world that often places too much value on wealth and success, Mr. Dhoriya has shown us that the greatest treasures are found in the acts of kindness we extend to others. His life is a living example of how to live with purpose and compassion—a beacon for all who seek to make the world a better place through the quiet, steady practice of benevolence.

Through his example, Mr. Dhoriya has taught us that the true measure of a man is not found in what he accumulates, but in what he gives away—his time, his love, his knowledge, and his kindness. This is his legacy: a legacy that will continue to inspire generations to come, encouraging them to live not for themselves, but for others.

XVIII
Conclusion

A Life to Embrace and Embody

As you reach the final words of this book, take a moment to let its lessons settle in your heart. The life of Mr. Dhoriya is not just a story; it is a beacon of what is possible when a person commits to values that transcend personal gain—values like empathy, patience, integrity, lifelong learning, and service to humanity.

In an environment often marked by haste, competition, and division, this narrative offers a reminder that true fulfilment lies in fostering connections, uplifting others, and staying true to principles that build a better world. It challenges us to reflect on our own lives and ask: how can we, too, live with such purpose and impact?

Reflect Deeply on These Questions

- **Empathy**: Do I truly listen to others without judgment? How can I offer support to those in need, even when it requires personal sacrifice?
- **Integrity**: Am I consistent in my values, actions, and words, regardless of whether I'm seen or unseen?
- **Patience**: Do I endure life's trials with grace, trusting in the process and focusing on what I can control?
- **Lifelong Learning**: Am I committed to growing as a person, seeking knowledge and wisdom, and encouraging others to do the same?
- **Service**: How can I contribute to my family, community, and world in a way that leaves a lasting legacy of kindness and inspiration?

Practical Steps to Start Your Journey

This book calls you to action—to not just admire the values it embodies, but to live them. Here's how:

1. **Empathy in Action**

   - Practice daily acts of kindness: a smile to a stranger, a word of encouragement to a colleague, or a helping hand to someone struggling.
   - Listen without interrupting or judging. Seek to understand the emotions behind someone's words.

1. **Integrity as a Foundation**

- Set a personal standard of honesty in all areas of life. Keep your word, even when it's inconvenient.
- Reflect on your actions at the end of each day: Were they aligned with your values?

2. **Patience as Strength**

- When faced with adversity, pause. Breathe. Remind yourself that every challenge is temporary and holds a lesson.
- Practice gratitude for the present moment, focusing on progress rather than perfection.

3. **Lifelong Learning as a Habit**

- Dedicate time to learning something new every day. Read books, engage in meaningful conversations, or take up a skill you've always wanted to master.
- Share your knowledge with others—teaching is one of the most powerful ways to solidify your learning and inspire others.

4. **Service as a Legacy**

- Volunteer your time, resources, or skills to causes that resonate with your heart. Remember, no contribution is too small.
- Lead by example. Inspire your children, peers, and community to adopt values that uplift everyone.

Be a Ripple in the World

One person's actions may seem small, but they can create ripples that grow into waves of change. By choosing to live with purpose, as Mr. Dhoriya did, you contribute to a kinder, more connected world. Imagine the impact if everyone reading this book committed to just one value they found within these pages—how many lives could be touched?

A Personal Challenge

Take one lesson from this book that resonates most deeply with you, and commit to embodying it over the next month. Journal your experiences. Share your journey with others. Watch how your actions inspire those around you.

A Message of Hope

This is not a call for perfection. None of us will live without flaws or mistakes, and that's part of being human. But what matters is the intent to grow, to contribute, and to create a life that reflects the principles of compassion, resilience, and humility.

You have the power to become the kind of person whose life inspires others. You can be the teacher, the mentor, the friend, or the parent who makes others believe in their potential. Just as Mr. Dhoriya's life has touched yours, your life can touch countless others.

The world needs more individuals like him—people who choose to uplift rather than tear down, to give rather than take, and to lead by example. The journey starts with you.

Let this book be your guide, your motivation, and your call to action. Take the lessons you've read and transform them into a life that matters—a life that inspires, uplifts, and leaves a legacy for generations to come.

About The Author And The Book

Dr. Yagnesh N. Dhoriya

Dr. Yagnesh N. Dhoriya is an Assistant Professor of English at Tolani College of Arts and Science, Adipur-Kachchh, where he has been shaping young minds since 2015. A dedicated educator and writer, he believes in the power of storytelling to inspire and transform lives. This book is a heartfelt tribute to his father, Naranbhai Dhoriya, whose journey as an educator and a guiding force left a profound impact on many.

Naranbhai Dhoriya served as an Assistant Teacher of English at Seth D. V. High School in Anjar-Kachchh, dedicating his life to the noble cause of education. After years of service, he retired in 2021 and now enjoys a peaceful and fulfilling life in the small town he always called home. His story, though deeply personal, carries universal lessons of perseverance, integrity, and the power of education.

More than just a biography, this book aspires to be a source of motivation—a self-help narrative that may serve as a beacon of hope for those who have lost their way. Dr. Dhoriya does not know how the book will be received, but the desire to share this journey and spread its wisdom was one he could not ignore.